"This new series of books is
While Paul still continues to
collaborators, friends, and relations remain all too often in the dark
or are dealt with only incidentally. Yet giving proper consideration to
Paul's web of social relations can help us understand the Apostle
himself and his legacy."

—*God's Word Today*

"Trainor's little book makes an elusive character, mentioned only
three times in the New Testament, come to life. Through careful word
study he unlocks layers of meaning and presents sociological and
anthropological models in easily comprehensible language. The use
of network analysis enables the social networks implied in the
Letters to Philemon and the Colossians to be so illustrated that it
actually gives us something of a commentary on the two Letters.
Trainor effectively maintains the balancing act between various
positions on Pauline authorship. This study also illustrates some of
the breadth of the Lycus Valley project at Flinders University, which
is not confined to archaeology but expands to include all possible
aspects of ancient life there."

—*Carolyn Osiek*
Professor of New Testament
Brite Divinity School
Fort Worth, Texas

"Complementing his archaeological work at Colossae, Michael
Trainor here makes skillful use of insights from sociology and
cultural anthropology to cull a remarkable amount of information
concerning Paul's trusted co-worker Epaphras and the network of
churches that he founded and served in the Lycus Valley. While
accessible and rewarding for Bible study-groups in contemporary
parish communities, this study also offers a reliable—and I believe
unique—resource for scholars on a neglected but significant early
Christian leader."

—*Brendan Byrne, SJ*
Professor of New Testament
Jesuit Theological College
Parkville (Victoria), Australia

Paul's Social Network: Brothers and Sisters in Faith
Bruce J. Malina, Series Editor

Epaphras
Paul's Educator at Colossae

Michael Trainor

A Michael Glazier Book

LITURGICAL PRESS
Collegeville, Minnesota

www.litpress.org

A Michael Glazier Book published by Liturgical Press

Cover design by Ann Blattner. *Saint Paul,* fresco fragment, Roma, 13th century.

Unless otherwise indicated, all biblical translations are by the author.

The map of Asia Minor on p. x is from Henry Barclay Swete. *The Apocalypse of St John* (London: MacMillan, 1906).

The photograph of the stele on p. 17 is from MAMAVI.48. W. H. Buckler and W. M. Calder, *Monumenta Asiae Minoris Antiqua,* vol. 6 (Manchester: Manchester University Press, 1939), 18.

The photograph of the funerary stele on p. 18 is from MAMAVI.47. W. H. Buckler and W. M. Calder, *Monumenta Asiae Minoris Antiqua,* vol. 6 (Manchester: Manchester University Press, 1939), 17.

1   2   3   4   5   6   7   8   9

Library of Congress Cataloging-in-Publication Data

Trainor, Michael F., 1950–
        Epaphras : Paul's educator at Colossae / Michael Trainor.
              p.   cm. — (Paul's social network)
        "A Michael Glazier book."
        Includes bibliographical references (p.   ) and indexes.
        ISBN 978-0-8146-5230-5 (pbk.)
        1. Epaphras (Biblical figure).   2. Paul, the Apostle, Saint—
Friends and associates.   I. Title.

BS2452.E63T73 2008
227'.7092—dc22

                                                                2008037070

CONTENTS

Chapter 7

Summarizing Epaphras of Colossae   93

Notes   97

Bibliography   109

Index of Person and Subjects   116

Index of Biblical Sources   121

Illustrations

PREFACE

uman beings are embedded in a set of social relations. A social network is one way of conceiving that set of social relations in terms of a number of persons connected to one another by varying degrees of relatedness. In the early Jesus group documents featuring Paul and coworkers, it takes little effort to envision the apostle's collection of friends and friends of friends that is the Pauline network.

This set of brief books consists of a description of some of the significant persons who constituted the Pauline network. For Christians of the Western tradition, these persons are significant ancestors in faith. While each of them is worth knowing by themselves, it is largely because of their standing within that web of social relations woven about and around Paul that they are of lasting interest. Through this series we hope to come to know those persons in ways befitting their first-century Mediterranean culture.

Bruce J. Malina
Creighton University
Series Editor

INTRODUCTION

When I returned to South Australia after a time of study leave from Flinders University's school of theology where I teach, colleagues and friends invariably asked what I had been working on. My response was, among other things, that I had begun to write on Epaphras. The silent response from my inquirers meant that they were trying to work out who or what "Epaphras" was: perhaps the name of an ancient disease, part of a Greek verb, the title of a little-known land in the Mediterranean basin, or some fictitious character of ancient literature. In the pages ahead I will show how Epaphras was a central figure in the growth of Jesus movement groups in an area known as the Lycus Valley, situated in the Roman province of Asia. Today the region is in southwestern Turkey, about an hour's flight from Istanbul. As we shall see, Epaphras was a companion of Paul who presented and explained the Gospel of God to the Jesus groups in Colossae.

My interest in Epaphras has emerged in the context of an interdisciplinary project initiated in the school of theology of Flinders University, South Australia, about a decade ago to interpret archaeologically the unexcavated site of ancient Colossae. Together with colleagues from the university, in particular Associate Professor Claire Smith and Dr. Alan Cadwallader, we established research partnerships with Turkish archaeologists Professor Dr. Çelal Şimşek and Professor Dr. Bilal Sögüt of Pamukkale University, Denizli, the university nearest to Colossae. Çelal and Bilal have fruitfully excavated sites in the Lycus Valley

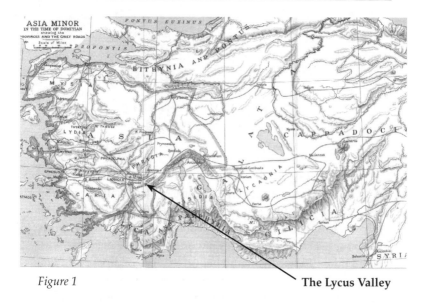

Figure 1   **The Lycus Valley**

and surrounding areas. In particular, Çelal has worked on the two other ancient cities associated with the valley, Hierapolis and Laodicea, directing the archaeological interpretation of the latter. Over the years friendship and commitment to the project have grown between all of us. The future archaeological interpretation of Colossae looks promising and, we hope, will reveal insights that will help us better understand the cultural and religious contexts of the two Pauline letters associated with the valley, the letter to Philemon and the letter to the Colossians.

I am grateful to many for the critique and suggestions offered on earlier drafts of this book. Doctoral students Joan Riley and Rosemary Canavan suggested fruitful lines of investigation from their particular research interests and commitment to the Colossae project. My colleague Dr. Marie Turner read an early draft and offered sagacious comments that helped clarify the methodological underpinnings of this study. I am especially appreciative of the helpful critique offered by Bruce Malina, whose encyclopedic knowledge on things cultural and anthropological saved me from many anachronistic blunders. I owe a great debt of thanks to Alan Cadwallader for his help in elucidating positions I take on Epaphras and his world. Alan also generously gave me access to his most recent work on funerary stele inscriptions pertinent to the Lycus Valley and Colossae. These inscriptions have helped me fill out chapter 2 and the network friendship pattern prominent in the time of Epaphras and the writer of the letter to the Colossians.

Finally, I have been aware of the Catholic community of Elizabeth, South Australia, as I reflected on the educational role of Epaphras for the Jesus households of the Lycus Valley. My ministry among this contemporary Jesus household has helped me realize that what Epaphras did in the first century is what is needed in our contemporary church. To the Catholic parishioners of Elizabeth I dedicate this book and its story of Epaphras.

CHAPTER 1

Introducing Epaphras

Epaphras was a respected companion of Paul. He taught Paul's Gospel of God to Jesus groups in southwest Asia Minor, in an area known as the Lycus Valley, now in today's Turkey. Epaphras is not remembered like Timothy or Silvanus, who readily come to mind as Paul's companions. His is not a popular name today, like Timothy. In fact, I cannot even think of anyone called Epaphras! He is one of Paul's forgotten collaborators, a fact further confirmed by the few references to "Epaphras" in the New Testament. This specific form of his name occurs only in two Pauline letters, Philemon and the letter to the Colossians, for a total of three references (Col 1:7; 4:13; Phlm 23). With three mentions in the New Testament, the task of writing a book about him becomes quite a challenge.

When we delve into Philemon and Colossians several helpful insights emerge concerning Epaphras' location and description in these letters that likewise assist in situating him against the background of the Greco-Roman Mediterranean world. This book is an attempt to summarize these insights. As I draw upon the contributions from cultural and anthropological studies and look closely at the documents themselves, elements of a remarkable portrait of Epaphras materialize: his relationship with the apostle Paul, his importance for early Jesus household gatherings in Asia Minor, especially at Colossae, the strength of a deeply committed faith leader, a theological depth shaped by the religious convictions of Paul, and a third- or fourth-generation disciple of Jesus embedded in the cultural world of late first-century CE Asia Minor. Sensitivity to the cultural patterns and social values that permeated the world of Paul and Epaphras will further help us understand the relationships Paul and the writer to the Colossians had to those to whom they were writing. It will also help deepen our appreciation of Epaphras' activity among the Pauline household gatherings of the Lycus Valley and his relationship with Paul and his colleagues. Other aspects about Epaphras' role will also emerge from a careful reading of the letters themselves.

There are two key insights I rely upon in the pages ahead. Though well explicated elsewhere, these insights are best summarized here, given their importance and influence on our story of Epaphras.[1] They concern:

- The nature of the "genuine" Pauline letters and the identity of the writer of Colossians

- The "high-context" quality of the New Testament writings

The Writers of Philemon and Colossians

First, while there is still some ongoing scholarly discussion about this, I regard seven letters among Paul's writings as indisputably coming from his hand. These are 1 Thessalonians, 1 and 2 Corinthians, Philippians, Galatians, Romans, and Philemon. Our chronologically earliest exposure to Epaphras in Philemon comes from Paul himself. The remaining Pauline letters are certainly authentic letters in the New Testament collection of writings. They were inspired by Paul's spirit and teaching, and in an indirect sense can also be considered "genuine." But there is no consensus as to who actually wrote them. This non-authentic collection includes the letter to the Colossians.

There are several reasons for this question mark over the identity of the writer of Colossians. For one thing, the changed Christ-rooted perspectives on eschatology, ecclesiology, Christology, and baptism in Colossians differ from the undisputed letters of Paul. Further indication of non-Pauline origin are the presence of terms found nowhere else in the New Testament and the absence of expected phrases and words obvious in those letters Paul wrote.[2] These differences in Colossians are significant and cannot be explained by a "development hypothesis" that attributes the differences in the disputed Pauline letters, including Colossians, to maturation in Paul's thinking about Jesus Christ. Along with others I consider that Colossians was not personally written by Paul himself, but penned after his death by a disciple of Paul writing in his name.

Paul belonged to the second and the writer of Colossians to the third or fourth generation of Jesus followers.[3] This writer wanted Paul's voice to speak "from the grave" to new pastoral situations in Jesus gatherings he founded or for which he was responsible. The letter to the Colossians comes from a later generation of Jesus followers responding to issues more cosmic and universal in scope, unforeseen by Paul himself. Though Paul was not the writer of Colossians in the direct sense, he was so indirectly. His spirit, interpreted for a new generation of Jesus followers by Epaphras, influenced the teaching that permeates the letter, in which its writer urges fidelity to Paul's original baptismal vision now reinterpreted for new circumstances.

If Paul did not write the letter, then who did? Epaphras' authoritative teaching status is clearly affirmed in Colossians 1. This affirmation has suggested to some that perhaps Epaphras was its writer.[4] The honor Paul shows to Epaphras allows the letter's hearers to respect Epaphras and attend to his teaching. This is particularly pertinent if Paul's death has precipitated a crisis over leadership in the Jesus gatherings of the region. What was needed was a person who might stabilize and prevent discontinuance of Paul's gospel, while presenting a correct interpretation of Paul's teaching for the next generation of Jesus followers.[5] If Epaphras is the letter's writer, then the letter is written for a third generation of Jesus followers. In this scenario Epaphras confirms the transition to the next stage of Jesus group leadership and provides a balancing, tempering voice of stability in an unsettling time.

A further writing scenario might also be possible. The strong support and affirmation "Paul" gives to Epaphras in Colossians might also be conceivable at a time when the credibility of Epaphras' interpretation of Paul has been seriously brought into question. It would come from those whose understanding about Jesus and his authority over the cosmic powers had been sidelined and branded in error by Epaphras. I shall examine the nature of this crisis in the Colossian Jesus assemblies later, but those targeted by Epaphras would seize an opportunity to retaliate against his criticism. A most opportune moment for this retaliation would present itself when Epaphras was no longer around to defend his application of Paul's teaching. This would naturally occur after his death. In this second scenario the letter to the Colossians represents a reaffirmation of Epaphras' interpretation of Paul by a *fourth*-generation Jesus follower schooled in Paul's teaching as presented by his faithful companion, Epaphras.

Whatever the identity of the writer of Colossians, its chronological positioning after Paul himself offers an opportunity to study Epaphras' legacy across at least two generations of Jesus followers. We can compare Epaphras' portrait in the letter to Philemon with his portrayal in Colossians. The first comes from Paul's own hand; this is the Epaphras of the historical Paul of the mid 50s CE. The Epaphras of the letter to the Colossians comes from the post-Pauline period of the 60s or 70s CE. This might be Epaphras' self-portrait (if he is the writer of Colossians, as some hold) or the portrait of a Pauline writer faithful to a heritage faithfully communicated through Epaphras at a time when Paul's teaching needed reinterpretation for a later generation of Jesus followers. The Colossian writer offers a study of Epaphras that we can compare and contrast with Paul's presentation of Epaphras in Philemon.

Social Context of Philemon and Colossians

Second, the letters to Philemon and Colossians presume information well-known to their audiences. This presumption indicates that the letters were written in a "high-context" society.[6] High-context societies produce sketchy and impressionistic texts, leaving much to the reader's or hearer's imagination. Since people believe few things have to be spelled out, few things are in fact spelled out. This is so because people have been socialized into shared ways of perceiving and acting, and therefore much can be assumed. What is communicated is understood by those who hear the letters. Detailed information does not have to be spelled out. The context of understanding is "high," that is, it is *highly* understandable.

On the other hand, our contemporary society is a "low-context" society. Low-context societies produce detailed texts, spelling out as much as conceivably possible, leaving little to the imagination. The general norm is that most things must be clearly set out: hence information must be continually added if meaning is to be constant. Such societies are fine-print societies, societies "of law" where every dimension of life must be described by legislators to make things "lawful." Modern Western readers tend to think all documents are low-context writings just like our own. Our "low-context" setting, chronologically and culturally distant from the original addressees of both letters, requires us to have the meanings of these high-context documents spelled out. Difficulties arise when we apply our literal and low-context understanding to writings that presume otherwise.

Relevant for our unfolding portrait of Epaphras and linked to this high-context presumption are two other cultural features worth exploring, the group-centered nature of Epaphras' world and the social meaning of Epaphras' name. These clear the ground for us to investigate the pattern of social networks evident in the letters, on which their writers draw and into which Epaphras is inserted.

The Group-Centered Nature of Epaphras' World

A first feature is the group-centered nature of Epaphras' world. This cultural note is difficult for us, especially given our penchant for individualism, introspection, personality differences, and our desire for personal privacy. Our privacy is so important to us that we legislate to ensure that it is protected. We seek to comprehend what makes us so different from others that we rely on the Myers-Briggs personality profile or the Enneagram to help us to understand our uniqueness and why we do what we do.

All this would be strange to Epaphras and his colleagues. Their world was centered on others, what others thought about them and why they reacted in certain ways. The letters presume this collective group-centeredness. It is reflected in the cooperational rapport between Paul and his coworkers, the accreditation given to Epaphras for his teaching status, and the unity expressed to the letters' addressees through the greetings from Paul's colleagues.[7] Philemon and Colossians are addressed to Jesus-household assemblies and their members. They are not concerned about individual or private religious maturation. Paul's letter to Philemon, for example, is not directed exclusively or solely to the individual Philemon, but explicitly to Apphia, Archippus, and Philemon's Jesus-group household (Phlm 2).

Epaphras' Name

An appreciation of the group-centered nature of Epaphras' world also has implications for understanding Epaphras' name. Members of Epaphras' first-century Jesus assemblies would consider a person's name significant. A name communicated a world of meaning and relational identity. This is similar to, though different from, contemporary experience.

My first name is, of course, most precious to me. "Michael" identifies me individually and personally. It says who I am in myself; when I think of my name, I think of all those experiences—personal, cultural, and social—that have shaped me into the kind of person I am. My last name, "Trainor," says something of my Irish heritage and ancestry. The discovery that the original Irish spelling of my last name, "Traynor," was changed to "Trainor" when my adolescent great-great-grandfather came from County Wicklow in Ireland to Australia in the mid-nineteenth century says much about the political history represented in the name change and experienced by my forebears. The new, anglicized surname resulted from a need to accommodate to a dominant British colonial settlement in the Antipodes and simply to "get on" in a new world on the other side of the globe, far from Ireland.

In Epaphras' day a person's name symbolized the larger social or tribal group to which the person belonged. This is the network of relationships that typified Epaphras' Greco-Roman world and on which we shall reflect in greater depth next. Names given to people in this circum-Mediterranean culture of group consciousness linked people to their kinship group, tribe, and wider patterned network. It cemented the group identity that marked ingroups from outgroups rather than signifying an individuality that distinguished them from the group, as happens today. Kinship in this ancient context concerned the total social domain influenced by all familial transactions and relationships.[8] Names today act to distinguish and individualize. Ancient names *confirmed*, or in some instances, especially in the case of slaves, *imposed* tribal, kinship identity. Special significance was also associated with a name deriving from the name of one of the tribal gods. The derivation of ancient names from the pantheon of gods was not uncommon.[9] This is the case with "Epaphras."

"Epaphras" is a shortened form of "Epaphroditus," a name associated with the goddess Aphrodite.[10] This association with a prominent Greek deity suggests that Epaphras' predecessors were not Jesus followers. The Greek cultural heritage indicated by his name would imply that he was probably a Hellenized Israelite who joined some Jesus-movement group. The problem with the term "Greek" in the first-century Mediterranean is that it usually referred to one's social standing as a civilized person. The opposite of Greek was barbarian. What we call "Greece" today did not exist in the first century.

Epaphras might well represent a new generation of believers who emerged from a religiously diverse Israelite world. Further, Epaphras' authority, to which Paul and the writer of the letter to the Colossians attest, might also mirror the kind of status he was shown within his kinship group. This might further suggest that this kinship group, his primary familial household, located in Colossae, was also part of the Jesus movement. While Epaphras lived in Colossae, his proclamation of the Gospel of God and his interpretation of Paul's teaching also extend to other relatively closely intertwined Jesus-group households in the Lycus Valley, at Hierapolis, and at Laodicea.[11] This interrelationship is spelled out in Colossians, toward the end of the letter.

The frequency of the name "Epaphras" throughout the Mediterranean, especially in Asia Minor, is well known.[12] There is inscriptional evidence of the existence of both forms of the names, "Epaphras" and "Epaphroditus," before the Common Era, though it was more common in the imperial era. Both forms appear throughout the Mediterranean, especially in Macedonia, Achaia, Magna Graecia (southern Italy), and Sicily. Persons with these names are associated with a variety of occupations. The names come from a broad social cross section, from servile to elite, and include slaves, freedmen, benefactors, and, on at least one inscription from Ephesus, a priest of the imperial cult.[13] A majority of references in Magna Graecia (southern Italy) are to slaves, victims of Roman conquest forced into slavery irrespective of their original social status.

Given that evidence, it is possible that the Epaphras of Philemon and Colossians was a slave or a former slave, or he might have been a person of elite social standing. Apart from the name's predominant association with slaves, two other indicators from Philemon and Colossians tip the balance in favor of Epaphras' servile background.

First, slaves were integral to the domestic landscape and are presumed to have been members of Jesus households.[14] This is obvious in Philemon and from the rhetoric Paul employs in encouraging Philemon to welcome back his runaway slave Onesimus (Phlm 8-17). The appearance of Epaphras' name at the head of the list of those who send their greetings to Philemon (Phlm 23) would add further strength to Paul's appeal if Epaphras' background was servile, and provided Philemon accepted the honor of Epaphras' head position. Second, the extensive treatment given to slaves, who are directly addressed in the "household code" of Colossians 4:22-26, also presumes Jesus-group households that counted slaves among their membership. The writer positions the second mention of Epaphras not many verses after this code. Its emphatic appeal to slaves makes further sense if Epaphras was a former slave whom Paul supports as instructor to the Colossians.

Both forms of the name are also present in Paul's writings. While our attention is specifically on the Epaphras of Philemon and Colossians, some have suggested that he is the one Paul calls "Epaphroditus" in Philippians 2:25 and 4:18. In the two genuine Pauline letters where Epaphroditus and Epaphras occur, Philippians and Philemon, Paul does not use the forms of these names interchangeably in the same letter. This is because they are distinct and separate colleagues in a ministerial entourage with different services in different locations. Epaphras is associated with the Lycus Valley of southwest Asia Minor, Epaphroditus with Macedonia (that is, with what is northern Greece today). This would also explain Paul's different description of them in each letter.

In Philippians 2:25, Epaphroditus is described as "my brother and fellow worker and fellow soldier, and your apostle and minister of my needs." In Philemon 23, Paul simply names Epaphras as "my fellow prisoner in Christ Jesus." The expanded description for Epaphroditus accounts for his role among the Philippians. He is Paul's fellow laborer ("fellow soldier") who struggles with Paul in a mutual task, is Paul's messenger ("apostle") and fulfills a quasi-liturgical role ("minister") among the Philippians. Paul's description of Epaphras as "fellow prisoner in Christ Jesus" underscores this person's solidarity with Paul in his struggles in Christ. It is this solidarity that accredits Epaphras' greetings to Paul's addressees in the letter's final verses. More will be said of this later as we investigate the Epaphras of Philemon in greater detail.

There is a final point to consider before we conclude our discussion of the Pauline use of the names Epaphras and Epaphroditus. The description the post-Pauline writer of Colossians gives of Epaphras reflects none of the terms Paul uses of Epaphroditus. The only similarity between these two characters is their role as Paul's envoys to their respective communities. Epaphroditus is Paul's delegate, who represents the concerns of the Philippians back to Paul. By comparison, Epaphras' role as instructor and interpreter of Paul's Gospel of God, as well as his authoritative status among the Colossians, appears more elevated. He is strongly connected to members of the Colossian Jesus-group through a variety of network relationships, the focus of the next chapter.

CHAPTER 2

Epaphras' Social Network

The writings of the New Testament are faithful reflections on the activities of the God of Israel in the story of Jesus (as in the case of the gospels) and its implications (as in Paul's letters) for later Jesus assemblies. They are also literary and cultural artifacts that reflect the social world in which they are written. They reflect the collectivist spirit and social orientation described above. These societal cultural values also permeate Philemon and Colossians, which reflect the relationship patterns typical of Asia Minor and presumed by Paul in Philemon and by the writer of Colossians. These reveal themselves through a closer study of the network patterns that lay behind Paul's descriptions of his colleagues and the rhetoric of relationships echoed in each letter's greetings and farewells. Their writers reveal a range of relationships shaped by status, honor, friendship, and patronage that Paul has with his associates, Epaphras, and those addressed by the letters. The range of linguistic descriptors used by Paul in Philemon and "Paul" in Colossians can help explicate this network pattern.

When the usual caveat is applied, contemporary network analysis can assist in locating Epaphras within Paul's network of relationships and his relationship, later, to the Lycus Valley Jesus assemblies. The caveat referred to here is that used in biblical social science perspectives that caution against retrojecting contemporary theories and abstractions onto an earlier period with little appreciation of historical distance and cultural difference or social sensitivity. This links to the caution Moses I. Finley offers regarding the use of models derived from a contemporary context and applied to a different historical scenario.[1] He writes:

> It is the nature of models that they are subject to constant adjustment, correction, modification or outright replacement. . . . [T]here is virtually nothing that cannot be conceptualized and analyzed by non-mathematical models—religion, ideology, economic institutions and ideas, the state and politics, simple descriptions and developmental sequences. The familiar fear of a-priorism is misplaced: any hypothesis can be modified, adjusted or discarded when necessary. Without one, however, there can be no explanation; there can be only reportage and crude taxonomy, antiquarianism in its narrowest sense.[2]

The model(s) network analysis theory provided for understanding relationships among first-century Jesus-group members cannot be used in a prescriptive manner but must be adjusted and modified, as Finley suggests. Network analysis can be helpful only insofar as it can contribute to a description of Epaphras' social networks. That is, such analysis can provide a framework to help elucidate the pattern of relationships presumed in Philemon and Colossians and in which Epaphras is involved. This pattern can in turn help to identify Epaphras' unique role at Colossae and in the Lycus Valley.

Social Network Analysis

Social network analysis has been helpful to biblical scholars looking for ways to better understand the web of interconnectivity and pattern of relationships evident among persons described in the New Testament writings.[3] Network analysis developed in the mid-twentieth century in a complex history represented in three traditions: sociometric analysis employing graph theory to study small groups, the 1930s Harvard study of interpersonal relations and "cliques," and the work of Manchester anthropologists who applied sociometric analysis and the Harvard interpersonal analysis to understand the structure of tribal and village communities. These three strands were eventually forged in the 1960s and 1970s into a systematic approach to social network analysis.[4] An early key figure in the promotion and accessibility of network analysis was J. A. Barnes. His fieldwork in a fishing village in southwest Norway helped him highlight the main integrating factors of community life that were independent of the traditional anthropological concepts of geography, economics, or politics. These were *kinship, friendship,* and *neighborhood ties* or *association.* These primordial relations established what Barnes called a "network":

> Each person is, as it were, in touch with a number of people, some of whom are directly in touch with each other and some of whom are not. . . . I find it convenient to talk of a social field of this kind as a network. The image I have is of a set of points some of which are joined by lines. The points of the image are people, or sometimes groups, and the lines indicate which people interact with each other.[5]

Barnes' network presumes personal interactions that create a "social field" of friendship. He images the interactions as lines that lead to points and represent people or groups. The work of Barnes and his Manchester colleagues has grown in many and complex directions as social researchers have taken the basic concepts of network analysis and applied them in the study of social structures, interpersonal networks, and structural analysis. Barnes' work had immediate application for European and American urban contexts. It has also been applied to rural and Mediterranean contexts.[6]

Network analysis will be helpful in sensitizing us to the emerging portrait of Epaphras across Philemon and Colossians and delineating how this portrait conforms to, yet departs from, the following expected pattern defined by analysts:[7]

1. *The network was established on relationships, usually asymmetrical, that differed in content and intensity.* The reciprocal contents of personal ties (information, goods, or power) were generally not the same. This lack of symmetry reflected the difference in content and intensity.

2. *The network linked its participants directly and indirectly, and ties must be studied in the larger context.* Some ties, like friendship, are voluntary; others (kinship, neighborhood, patron-client) are not.

3. *Structured social ties create purposeful networks, which form clusters, boundaries, and other social links.* Each person is linked into a variety of social networks, some of which form clusters. The various links people experience provide access to resources and the experience of solidarity.

4. *Asymmetric ties in networks mean that some control the resources that others need and that can be distributed differentially.* This is the basis of hierarchy and, especially in the ancient world, of retainers, "gatekeepers."

5. *Networks can encourage collaboration and competition as members seek to access resources.* This is the basis for collective political activity, structural change, and redistribution of resources.

The Patron-Client Relationship

Our focus on Epaphras will help identify the way these network principles operate in his interaction with Paul and others. This network pattern, viewed at a higher level of abstraction in Epaphras' society world, mirrored the patronage system of *cli-*

entela, well known in the Roman world: a person ("patron," usually though not exclusively a male) used status, goods, and power to advance or protect those of lower status ("clients"). This patron-client relationship was the earliest and most fundamental form of human relationship evident in the Roman Empire between the fifth century BCE and the fifth century CE.[8] It would have shaped relationships in Asia Minor, including the Lycus Valley and Colossae. The patron-client relationship was:[9]

—an *exchange relation* that involved a wide range of social interactions. The relationship was based on needs and wants. The client needed resources the patron could offer, usually practical and immediately tangible. These did not exclude the "resources" of friendship, inducements, and commitment. The client responded by honoring the patron, usually with intangible goods, through service, honoring the patron's name, and celebrating the favor shown;

—*materially expressed* and intimately linked to *loyalty and mutual solidarity.* It involved interpersonal obligation;

—*asymmetrical* and *hierarchical.* The parties were unequal in power, status, and resources. The resources exchanged varied according to the setting and could leave the client dependent on the patron for material provisions, mediation, or protection;

—*voluntary,* and it could be abandoned voluntarily, though usually it was considered long-term;

—*dyadic,* involving two or more other individuals or networks of individuals.

Though not all these aspects of patron-client interchange operated in every exchange and variations are known in the Roman world, the overall process could result in coercion on the part of the patron that would oblige the client to respond with honor. The exchange that originated out of inequality produced mutual solidarity that usually bound the client to the patron unconditionally.

This resulted in an interchange of benefits and obligations over a long time.

The pattern of social networks and the patron-client relationships fundamental to the networks are observable in Philemon and Colossians. They influenced the way the writers of the letters (Paul and "Paul") related to their addressees, portrayed Paul himself to his audience, and established Epaphras' importance to Philemon's Jesus group and his authority among the Colossian Jesus followers. When these cultural patterns and insights are placed alongside the particular network foci first formulated by Barnes, a helpful template emerges that we can now use as we begin to study the letters, their description of Epaphras, and the network patterns that shaped his portrait. As this portrait surfaces I will suggest, by means of a close reading of the descriptors the writers of Philemon and Colossians apply to Epaphras, how the above understanding of the social network pattern and patron-client relationship is presumed and adjusted.

Kinship, Friendship, and Neighborhood

My interest in Barnes' study is its immediate application to the social network patterns discernible in Philemon and Colossians. This is particularly obvious when Barnes' three core integrating network factors of *kinship, friendship,* and *neighborhood association* are used as interpreting metaphors. These three factors have their first-century CE Mediterranean equivalent. They are obvious in the relational, familial, and network language used by the writers of Philemon and Colossians. We shall look at this more closely in the next chapter. The importance of these relational metaphors to Greco-Roman society is also corroborated by funerary inscriptions. Of particular relevance are inscriptions from Colossae.

At present, research into Colossian inscriptions is in its infancy, yet it continues to expand as archaeological interest in the ancient site grows.[10] There are two funerary inscriptions (out of a possible twenty-four) relevant to the present discussion. The first is dated approximately to the same period as the writing of our two Pauline letters; the second is from the third century CE. Though this latter inscription postdates the period in which we are most interested, it reflects the relational spirit evident in the letters, which was then memorialized in a later period.

Colossian Funerary Monuments

The first Colossian funerary stele is most significant. It was first discovered in the early twentieth century in modern Honaz, the town closest to ancient Colossae, but only recently has its full import been recognized. The stele depicts a funerary banquet scene with two reclining figures, probably husband and wife, with two small children seated on either side of the table, which contains food. Beneath the table is a dog. The child figure on the left of the table is a girl touching bread. The child figure on the right, touching the food on the table, is possibly a boy. The whole scene evokes the kind of household intimacy and relational network that would typify the Jesus groups of the Colossian *polis* and is reflected in Philemon's household addressed by Paul's letter. A possible translation of the inscription under the scene reads:

Figure 2
Honaz Stele

> The youngest members of the clan (*syngenikon*)
>
> for Tatianos son of Tatianos grandson of Artas.[11]

The Greek *syngenikon* ("of the clan") is a sepulchral term, though not exclusively. It describes those responsible for erecting the funerary monument, namely, the clan or kin group representative of at least three generations. While the funerary scene and its inscription are not unique in the Greco-Roman world nor in Asia Minor, they are the only ones we have for the Lycus Valley and Colossae. They are contemporaneous with the Pauline letters and underscore the importance of familial intimacy and kinship responsibility for the deceased members of the clan that is memorialized for those who pass by this funerary monument.

The second funerary stele depicts two standing figures, a male and a female, similarly clothed, with the woman dressed in an unusual crinkled dress under her outer garment. The inscription on this stele is divided into two parts, separated by the figures. The upper line and the lines below the figures read:

> Greetings to those who pass /
> The society of friends (*hetairoi*)
> honor Gluko.[12]

Figure 3
Hetairoi Stele

Though dated to the third century CE, the monument is significant for its description of those who erected the memorial. They are called *hetairoi* and form an association or "society of friends." The definite article "the" before *hetairoi* is most noteworthy. In the early Greek period predating the Pauline corpus, *hetairos* was well known as a description of friends. By the third century CE and the carving of this inscription, "the" het-

airoi had become recognized as an association with a corporate identity. This means that the kind of network relationship known in the first century CE and reflected in Philemon and Colossians had by this time been legally formalized.

These two funerary monuments memorialized the role played by kinship and friendship. Such monuments were also intended to impress those who passed by. They likewise invite us to consider the role played by honor, status, the domestic setting, and the *polis* or *civitas* in constructing the network pattern.[13] All these were powerful social forces and settings that shaped the way people related to each other.

The Lycus Valley Network Pattern

The network pattern in each of the Jesus groups addressed by the letters would not be limited to one household assembly but would mirror similar patterns in other Jesus assemblies of the Lycus Valley to which all Jesus-group members were linked. The pattern could also be more complex, being influenced by other political, geographical, economic, cultural, and political factors that shaped daily life in the valley. The possibility of such

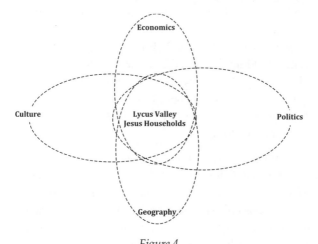

Figure 4
Network Pattern of Jesus Groups in the Lycus Valley

complexity points to an "infinite network" in which the complexity of relationships among all persons in a network is studied from the point of view of a total system (the "total network") and a universal, all-inclusive, unbounded network is established.[14]

Such a network description is beyond what I plan to focus on here. I envisage a more limited and partial network observable in Philemon and Colossians. If we return to Barnes' emphasis on *kinship*, *friendship*, and *neighborhood association*, we note that in the background lies the patron-client dynamic that helps to highlight the essential aspects of Paul's relationships with his colleagues and Epaphras' emerging role in Colossians. I hope to establish the nature of the patron-client dynamic and the social network pattern that involved and influenced Epaphras. I shall do this through a careful study of

1. the household setting both letters presume. This involves a focus on the *domestic network*, the centrality of the household in shaping the Pauline strategy and defining more specifically Epaphras' ministry within this domestic setting;

2. the language and character descriptors employed in the letters. I will pay particular attention to the specific language used in both letters, especially relational expressions and descriptions. My deeper intention is to unravel the *kinship-friendship network* that lies behind the personal language the writers of Philemon and Colossians use to speak of Paul, his relationships to others, and the unique language used of Epaphras. This will further involve reflections on the *patron-client dynamic* presumed by Paul and his coworkers in Philemon and Colossians;

3. the relationship of the household to the ancient *polis* of Colossae, and Colossae to the other cities of the Lycus Valley. This awareness of the *geographical* or *spatial network* insofar as this is possible will help add another dimension in refining the context of Epaphras' activity.[15] My reflection on this spatial network will be offered toward the end of this book,

as I look more closely at the explicit geographical markers of Epaphras' ministry offered in the very last verse in which he is mentioned in the New Testament (Col 4:13).

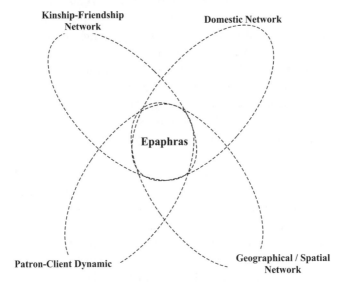

Figure 5
Epaphras' Networks

Paul in Philemon and Colossians

A cursory reading of the letters to Philemon and to the Colossians clearly indicates the centrality of the figure of Paul in both letters: he is their real or implied writer, first named and initial greeter of the addressees. His authority and status are obvious to all those mentioned in both letters. In terms of network patterns, two aspects are clear: Paul is the center of the relational network in both letters, though in Colossians the center moves explicitly through the auspices of the Pauline writer from Paul to Epaphras, with "Paul" appropriately retaining overall authority; second, Paul's authority is explicit because of the potential

conflict or tension the letter addresses (in the case of Philemon
the conflict between members of a Jesus household, and in Colossians the tension brought about by some ignoring Paul's
original teaching in favor of a more local, Phrygian, tribal com-
posite preoccupied with astral angelology). In terms of social
network theory, the letters reveal an "ego-centered network," a
relational network that is focused specifically on *one person* (*egō*
in Greek means "I," the first person pronoun). This network
involves those (called in network theory "alters," meaning "others") who esteem Paul and over whom Paul has authority. He
is depicted as the relational center of the network; all relationships radiate out from him in a unidirectional and asymmetrical
manner.

In this ego-centered network that variation in relationships
can be illustrated through a series of concentric circles, with each
circle representing different orders or zones of intimacy.[16] This
diagramatic representation of the ego-centered network is helpful for viewing the various relationships of Jesus-group members
to Paul that emerge in Philemon and Colossians, as represented
in the zones of intimacy. Timothy occupies the first zone of in-

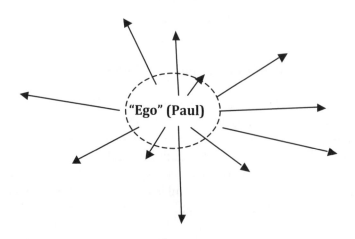

Figure 6
Paul's "Ego-centered Network"

timacy: he is named immediately after Paul mentions himself (Phlm 1; Col 1:1). Though Paul is the explicit or implicit writer of the letters, Timothy is also Paul's acknowledged co-sender. The next zone, the zone of the "effective network" in these Pauline letters, is constituted by those addressed. In Philemon they are Philemon and his household (Phlm 1b-2); in Colossians, "the saints and faithful brothers and sisters in Christ in Colossae" (Col 1:2a). "Extended networks," close to this second effective network zone but increasingly more distant, link Paul to those not directly addressed by the letters but who are in association or in a network with those addressed.

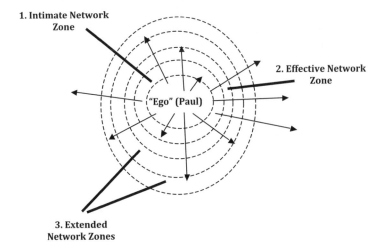

Figure 7
Networks Surrounding Paul

Network theory presumes that the variations in behavior of people in any one role relationship may be traced to the effects of the behavior of other people to whom they are linked in one, two, or more steps, in some other quite different relationships.[17] The zone differentials allow for this variation in behavior and response to Paul by all auditors of the letters and those outside the immediacy of the letters' intended audience who are also linked in different ways to those addressed or intended by the letters. In the next chapter, when we look more closely at the letter to Philemon, we shall see how Paul addresses an explicitly domestic network setting that reflects the "extended network zone." This audience, like those addressed in Colossians, is invited into the closer "intimate network zone." When we turn our attention to Colossians later we will find that the extended network zones are more complex. They include those Jesus-group households from Laodicea and Hierapolis explicitly mentioned in Colossians 4 that are the focus of Epaphras' activity. They also indirectly include those responsible for the factional and erroneous ritual practices influencing those immediately addressed by the writer ("effective network zone") implied in Colossians 2:4, 8, 16-23.

CHAPTER 3

The Domestic Network in the Letter to Philemon

iblical commentators generally agree that Paul wrote the letter to Philemon of Colossae around the mid-50s CE, when he was under arrest in Ephesus.[1] The frequent use of imprisonment and military imagery throughout this short letter, with Paul's unique self-designation in Philemon 1 as "prisoner" would support this context.

The standard Pauline greeting begins with the mention of Paul and Timothy as co-senders of the letter who greet the addressees, specifically Philemon, but also important members of his household:

> Paul, a prisoner of Christ Jesus, and Timothy our brother.
> To Philemon, our beloved one and coworker,
> Apphia our sister, and Archippus our fellow soldier,
> and the assembly in your household. (Phlm 1-2)

The familial terms Paul uses here (especially "brother" and "sister") and the explicit mention of the "assembly in your household" underscore the domestic network of the letter's addressees.

This network is presumed in the rest of the letter. How it differs from the conventional understanding of the household in wider Greco-Roman society remains to be seen. This appreciation must be the starting point for our subsequent discussion about the domestic network that shaped Philemon's household and, later, for the Jesus households addressed by Colossians. While we cannot presume that every Jesus group household was uniform in its dependents, a number of features about this domestic network are important to consider.[2]

The Domestic Network

First, the Greek contribution to Paul's understanding of the domestic network begins with the philosophical premise of the dyadic nature of the human person as a "political" and "social" being. Pythagoras (born ca. 570 BCE), Plato (428–348 BCE), and Aristotle (384–322 BCE) regarded every person as so influenced by society that his or her identity was communally related. Membership in the city-state meant that the city-state fashioned people's identity. Likewise, the household played an important and indispensable role in shaping the identity of its inhabitants. Plato and Aristotle identified the cardinal qualities foundational for the city-state and its primary component, the household. For Plato it was "order," for Aristotle, "partnership."

Plato believed that order was at the heart of the universe, and that the cosmos reflected in the city-state and its households was unattainable without the virtues of *communion, friendship, justice,* and *temperance.* In his important work *Gorgias,* Plato wrote:

> . . . where there is no communion, there can be no friendship. And the wise tell us that heaven and earth and gods and humans are held together by communion and friendship, by orderliness (*kosmiotēs*), temperance and justice; and this is the reason, my friend, why they call the whole world by the name of order (*kosmos*), not of disorder (*akosmia*) or dissoluteness.[3]

These two sentences are an important summary of Plato's political and domestic philosophy. Social and domestic order depended on the social virtues: communion, friendship, orderliness, temperance, and justice. All this had implications for households in which order was essential. In a dialogue between Socrates and Callides, Plato reminded his audience that "if regularity and order are found in a house, it will be a good one, and if irregularity, a bad one."[4]

In the opening to his major work, *Politics*, Aristotle wrote:

> Every city-state (*polis*) is as we see a sort of partnership (*koinōnia*), and every partnership is formed with a view to some good (since all the actions of everyone are done with a view to what they think to be good). It is therefore evident that, while all partnerships aim at some good, the partnership that is most supreme of all and includes all the others does so most of all, and aims at the most supreme of all goods; and this is the partnership entitled the city-state (*polis*), the political partnership.[5]

From this passage it is clear that Aristotle placed great importance on "partnership" (*koinōnia*). In his political philosophy *koinōnia* was a form of collective harmony that looked to the good or welfare of those who formed the city-state. Every social institution, including the household, was to be infused with it. It was the glue of society, a point not lost on later Roman writers.[6]

To ensure order and partnership, Plato and Aristotle argued for the perpetuation of patriarchal institutions based on relationships of domination-submission. They reinforced their argument for this institutional hierarchy from a model of humanity that presented the male as naturally superior and the female inferior. Aristotle further confirmed the importance of this hierarchy and subordination in his discussion on "household management" (*oikonomia*):

> Household management (*oikonomia*) falls into departments corresponding to the parts of which the household in its turn is composed. The primary and smallest parts of the

> household are master and slave, husband and wife, father
> and children; we ought therefore to examine the proper
> constitution and character of each of these three relation-
> ships, I mean that of mastership, that of marriage—there
> is no exact term denoting the relation uniting wife and
> husband—and thirdly the progenitive relationship—this
> too has not been designated by a special name.[7]

A brief review of Greek domestic philosophy also illustrates
the strong influence of the description of household relationships
in terms of domination-subordination and superiority-inferiority.
This was also the paradigm that controlled the description of
Jesus groups familiar to Paul and Philemon, since these groups
were "house churches," that is, fictive kinship groups modeled
after the household. The superior-inferior relationships that
concerned the management (*oikonomia*) of the Greek household—
the relationships between master and slave, husband and wife,
and father and children—determined the structure and order of
the domestic network. The kind of authoritarian structure presumed here also relied on an attitude of submissiveness. These
structures and attitudes existed at the time of the writing of
Philemon and Colossians and shaped the spirit of the domestic
network to which Paul and Epaphras belonged. The household's
stability reflected the order and stability desired of the wider
polis, the city-state. Order and "partnership" (*koinōnia*) guaranteed protection and security. This cultural context of the Lycus
Valley in southwest Asia Minor demanded that the households
of its three major cities, Hierapolis, Laodicea, and Colossae,
whether Jesus group households or not, reflect the kind of stability necessary for social cohesion and defense. This background
is presumed in the letter written to Philemon and his "high-
context" household at Colossae. It is further explicated in the
later letter to the Colossians, especially in the "household code"
reflected in Colossians 3:18–4:1.

The Domestic Network in Philemon

With this understanding of the domestic arena as a background we return to our consideration of Philemon. After Paul establishes the domestic setting for his letter with all the above allusions intended, Paul moves to engage Philemon with the implications of Onesimus' relationship to Paul and the need for Philemon to welcome Onesimus back into his household. In Philemon 9, Paul describes himself as an "elder" (*presbutēs*). This is a rhetorical fictional construction that places Paul as the "old man" to whom a fictive kinship honor and obedience were due. Paul concludes his appeal to Philemon by reminding him of the debt he owes Paul for his "own self" (v.19), of the confidence he has in Philemon's welcome of Onesimus (v. 21), and of Paul's impending visit to Philemon's household (v. 22). Then Paul ends with greetings from those with him, including Epaphras, and the final blessing: "The grace of the Lord Jesus Christ be with your spirit" (v. 25), typical of the conclusion in Paul's other letters (for example, Rom 16:20; 1 Cor 16:23; 2 Cor 13:13; Gal 6:18; Phil 4:23; 1 Thess 5:28) and an echo of the way he began his letter.

Apphia and Archippus are members of Philemon's household. In the letter's fictional construction their designations within the context of the "church" (an assembly, *ekklēsia*) that gathers in Philemon's house as "our sister" and "our fellow soldier" reflect the social network pattern indicated by the familial relationship characteristic of the household's fictive kinship, their common bond (which Paul expresses as *koinōnia* in the letter), and their role as his missionary companions.[8] The greeting illustrates the ego-centered network with Paul at its center. But alongside him is Timothy, Paul's "brother." He is one with Paul in writing to Philemon and his household and belonging to the first network zone of intimacy. The levels of authority in these opening verses reflect the asymmetrical and hierarchical nature of the network in which Philemon's Jesus household exists. Paul is the patron, acting as Onesimus' broker to Paul's clients in Philemon's household. But the terms of address Paul uses of Philemon and his household companions ("beloved one," "coworker," "our sister," "fellow soldier") already signal that changing nature of the conventional network pattern and the new criterion for patron-client relationships in the Jesus households.[9] This flags the movement of Philemon and his household to the closer second zone of intimacy in which Timothy already shares.

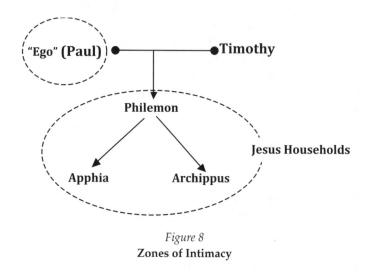

Figure 8
Zones of Intimacy

As the letter unfolds, Paul appeals to these addressees to welcome back Onesimus, who has run away from the household and is expecting to be severely reprimanded by Philemon for his conduct. Whether Onesimus is a runaway or a manumitted slave from the household or a bitterly estranged sibling is unclear, though scholarly weight favors the first view.[10] But he comes to Paul to intervene and orchestrate his acceptance back into Philemon's household. The relationship between Paul and Onesimus is close, and Paul responds on Onesimus' behalf: "I appeal to you about my child, whom I have begotten in chains, Onesimus" (v. 10).

Paul calls Onesimus "my child." He is not Paul's natural child, but one of Paul's new "converts" whom Paul "begat." This birthing image metaphorically describes Onesimus' baptismal experience, which resulted from Paul's prison instruction. The name "Onesimus" means useful, beneficial. Paul describes Onesimus as now no longer "useless" (*achrēstos*) to Philemon but "useful" (*euchrēstos*, v.11): Onesimus' status has changed from that of a nonbeliever in Philemon's household of believers ("useless") to that of a believer. This has happened through Paul's agency; because of him, Onesimus can be regarded as "useful" to Philemon's Jesus household. A few verses later Paul can refer to Onesimus as a "beloved brother" (v. 16). Onesimus' new baptismal status can challenge the hierarchical social conventions adopted by some and perhaps presumed in Philemon's household. Paul writes to remind Philemon of the nature of this renewed and different pattern of network relationships established in Christ through baptism.

This relationship established through baptism has implications for the sense of community in the Jesus group household. This relationship becomes the rhetorical basis for Paul's encouragement to Philemon to welcome Onesimus back as a brother "in the flesh and in the Lord" (v. 16). The rhetoric also builds upon and critiques the conventional patron-client relationship and social network patterns of the day. The relational implications obvious in the letter's opening verses, with their accompanying implicit social critique, provide the context from which we are now able to view Paul's presentation of Epaphras toward the letter's conclusion.

Greetings and Greeters (Philemon 23-24)

Greeters in Philemon 23-24

In Philemon 23-24 Paul includes greetings to Philemon from four people: Mark, Aristarchus, Demas, and Luke, with the list headed by the name of a fifth, Epaphras, his sole mention in all of Paul's genuine letters:

> [23] Epaphras, my fellow prisoner in Christ Jesus, sends greetings to you, [24] and so do Mark, Aristarchus, Demas, and Luke, my fellow workers. (Phlm 23-24)

Paul mentions Epaphras first in the list of greeters, his "fellow workers." This list and the opening greeting formula (Phlm 1-2) act as a frame within which the letter's rhetorical strategy unfolds. Paul's network of close colleagues surrounds the appeal he makes to Philemon. Their description ("brother," "fellow prisoner," "fellow workers") reveals the intimate network zone they occupy with Paul. Epaphras' prominence in the final list and the specific language Paul uses of him ("sends greetings") are noteworthy. His significance here becomes the catalyst the writer of the letter to the Colossians will draw upon and develop later.

Epaphras' "Greetings" to Philemon

When Paul comes to the greetings of the five in verses 23 and 24, Epaphras is particularly prominent. He is the first listed and is especially noted as offering a greeting to Philemon that is different from those of the others.

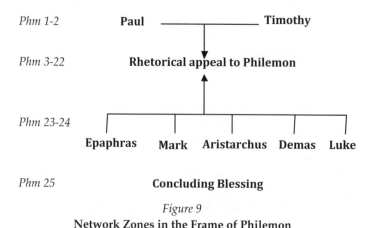

Figure 9
Network Zones in the Frame of Philemon

> Epaphras, my fellow prisoner of war greets (*aspazomai*) you
> in Christ Jesus, as do Mark, Aristarchus, Demas, and Luke,
> my fellow workers. (Phlm 23-24)

Paul's particular verbal form of Epaphras' greeting (*aspazomai*) is distinct in ancient Greek letters and, significantly, is conveyed to Philemon in the singular.[11] The same style of address that Paul uses to Philemon (Phlm 1) is also claimed for Epaphras. This suggests several things: First, Epaphras holds significant ranking and status for the addressees of the letter, similar to Paul's. His authority is affirmed and endorsed by Paul himself. Second, Ephaphras' greeting is quite similar to Paul's. This indicates a similar close relationship between Paul and Epaphras; it is a friendship, as we shall see below, founded on their relationship "in Christ." Finally, the greeting expresses the kind of relationship that reflects the intimate network zone Epaphras shares with Paul, Philemon, and the Jesus group that "meets in his house" (v. 1).

The greeting was important in ancient letters. The basic meaning of the Greek word was "to embrace." This ritual act invited a change of status as each person moved into the personal space of the other. It expressed sincerity of friendship and strengthened the personal bond of communion that had been affected by the separation caused by distance.[12] Within the Mediterranean of Epaphras' day, the greeting was an important ceremony, and within the gospel tradition it became one of the essential actions disciples were encouraged to perform when they entered households (Matt 10:12-13; Luke 10:5). The disciples' act of greeting on entrance into a house ensured peace upon the householders who showed the disciples hospitality. The greeting was accompanied by the gift or "power" of peace that is found in the New Testament tradition.[13] In Luke's journey narrative (in Luke 10:4), for example, the greeting was a deliberate, conscious act on the part of the disciples who were sent to proclaim the Gospel of God. The greeting was not something haphazard or accidental, intended for anyone on the journey. The significance of the greeting as a means to affirm the revelation of God's presence communicated by the greeter illustrates the special effort to expand and redefine the ancient virtue of hospitality with a perspective thought typical of Jesus.[14]

The greeting adopted in all the genuine letters of Paul was God-centered and emphatic. It communicated Paul's desire that the addressees of his letters would deeply experience God's presence and peace. This is also the case in his letter to Philemon, though with a slight difference. Rather than Paul *explicitly* offering the greeting customary in his other letters, Epaphras is the privileged closing greeter. The ideological depth of Epaphras' greeting at the end of the letter can only be appreciated by comparing the meaning of Paul's *implicit* greeting signaled in the letter's opening salutation (Phlm 3) with the blessing echoed in the final verse (Phlm 25):

> Grace to you and peace from God our Father and the Lord Jesus Christ. (Phlm 3)

> The grace of the Lord Jesus Christ be with your spirit. (Phlm 25)

Paul's Implicit Greeting (Philemon 3)

The sentence in Philemon 3 presents the explicit agenda of Paul's letter in a highly compact formula familiar in his other letters (Rom 1:7; 1 Cor 1:3; 2 Cor 1:2; Gal 1:3; Phil 1:2; 1 Thess 1:1). The greeting communicated more than the standard Greek *chairein*. Paul's "grace . . . and peace" in Philemon 3 linguistically and notionally expand on the conventional greeting, adding a dimension confirmed in his encounter with the risen Jesus.[15] This is the experience of God's *shalom*, a divine gift showered on God's people revealing the fullness of personal, social, cosmic, and heavenly communion. Paul's linking of "grace" and "peace" reflects elements of the priestly blessing uttered by the clan of Aaron over the Israelite people:[16]

> May the Lord bless you and keep you;
> May the Lord make his face shine upon you;

> May the Lord be gracious to you;
> May the Lord lift up his countenance on you and give you
> peace. (Num 6:24-26)

If Paul intends this link with the blessing in the book of Numbers in his opening formula and in the concluding line in Philemon, then "grace" takes on an even richer meaning. It concerns God's merciful, bounteous, covenantal love revealed through Jesus.[17] "Peace" is more than a personal sense of inner tranquillity in a troubled world. Rather, it concerns the fruit of the spirit of communion and well-being that emerges from God's relationship with Israel. Both expressions at the beginning of the letter emphasize the outcome of God's action revealed through Jesus Christ.

Apart from Paul's affirmation of Epaphras' status in the eyes of Philemon's household, the individuality and uniqueness of Epaphras' greeting presumes a close relationship with Philemon based in friendship and firmly established in their common faith "in Christ." Paul's greeting to Philemon and his household in Philemon 1-3, paralleled in Paul's conveyance of Epaphras' individual personal greeting in Philemon 23, illustrates the inclusive and close nature of the relationship of Paul, Epaphras, and Philemon (and his household). While the letter is in the first instance personally addressed to Philemon, the addition of other addressees in verse 2 (Apphia and Archippus and the "*ekklēsia*" that meets in Philemon's house) also means that the letter is a public document, typically collectivist, that is, intended for the wider audience that will inevitably hear about it. This suggests that the spirit of communion and friendship with Philemon implied through the specific style of greeting from Paul and Epaphras also includes the whole assembly, the *ekklēsia*, of Philemon's household.[18] All are united through the letter-event in a domestic network characterized by friendship and intimacy.[19]

The "Friendly" Letter

The renewal of social relationships and network negotiation is further underscored by a consideration of the nature of the greeting in the Greco-Roman letters of the period. As Cicero and Seneca noted, a writer of a letter addressed absent friends as though they were present.[20] This is also the case with Paul and Epaphras, as illustrated by their greetings. Paul's intention throughout the letter was to give encouragement. Its tone of friendship echoed in the greetings also reflected the convention of a "friendly letter," with its strong family ethos.[21]

Demetrius of Phaleron (ca. 350–ca. 280 BCE), in his handbook on letter writing, describes the friendly letter or letter of friendship (*philikai*) this way,

> The friendly type, then, is one that seems to be written by a friend to a friend. But it is by no means (only) friends who write (in this manner). For frequently those in prominent positions are expected by some to write in a friendly manner to their inferiors and to others who are their equals. . . . There are times when they write to them without knowing them (personally). They do so, not because they are close friends and have (only) one choice (of how to write), but because they think that nobody will refuse them when they write in a friendly manner, but will rather submit and heed what they are writing. Nevertheless, this type of letter is called friendly as though it were written to a friend. It is as follows: "Even though I have been separated from you for a long time, I suffer this in body only. . . ."[22]

The letter to Philemon reflects several elements of Demetrius' description of the friendly letter pattern. It is a letter written by a friend (Paul), from friends (Epaphras and the other greeters), to friends (Philemon and his household); the letter writer holds an authoritative position for those addressed in the letter; Paul authoritatively seeks to encourage Philemon to accede to his request for Onesimus; Paul also mentions his physical absence from Philemon—which will not last long because of Paul's intention to visit. Significantly, Philemon seems well known to Paul and Epaphras, and the letter presumes a deeper level of friendship that goes beyond mere acquaintanceship. For the next generation of Pauline letter writing in Colossians, Epaphras' friendship with Philemon and his household becomes the foundation for his authority among the Colossians. The friendship reflected in Philemon adds to its overall rhetorical strength. It confirms Paul's prominence as a patron of Onesimus and Philemon and gives further weight to his persuading appeal and argument to Philemon.

"Friendship" and "Union" (*koinōnia*) in Philemon

Paul's encouragement to Philemon neither remains nor stays on this level of relationship as defined by social convention and as prescribed by the patron-client pattern of relationship. Rather, it transcends the Greco-Roman patronage system through a richer appreciation of friendship. This draws upon and expands the notion of "friendship" and "union" as expressed in Cicero's description of the Roman household. The uniqueness Paul brings to this Roman understanding comes from the Christ-centered status of all in Philemon's household established through their "union" (*koinōnia*) with Jesus in baptism. This is further reflected through those who also send greetings to Philemon through Paul. Paul describes their status in terms of the common bond they share with Paul and his ministry. Their greetings, together with those of Epaphras, place further moral pressure on Philemon to respond affirmatively in the direction Paul has been encouraging throughout the letter. At the heart of everything is their common faith, their *koinōnia* in Jesus. Paul clearly spells this out in the letter:

> [I pray] that the communion (*koinōnia*) of your faith may
> be effective in the knowledge of all the good which is ours
> in Christ. (Phlm 6)

The content of Paul's prayer here adds another dimension to the greetings that come from Paul himself, his collaborators, and especially Epaphras. Paul describes himself in verse 7 as a *koinō-nos*, an agent of *koinōnia* with Philemon: "Therefore if you regard me as a *koinōnos*. . . ." Paul's self-description as *koinōnos* is difficult to translate. Most English versions suggest "partner" or "sharer."

In the world in which Paul writes, *koinōnia* reflected the spirit that undergirded the Roman concept of *societas*, a consensual social association characterized by trust, mutuality, and commitment. All those involved in the *societas* were partners committed to the shared goal for which the *societas* was established and were equal partners irrespective of social status or access to the material requirements to accomplish the goal.[23] This background is helpful in understanding Paul's use of *koinōnia* and *koinōnos* in Philemon.

Paul emphasizes the common bond of faith through their *societas* in Christ that Paul and Philemon share. Those who participate in this *societas* in mutuality and trust through their shared faith are called *koinōnoi*. Paul's use of this self-designation is a reminder to Philemon of Paul's ministry of deepening *koinōnia* within the Jesus community, of the faith communion they share in Jesus, and that together they are *koinōnoi*. What Paul is to the communities for which he is responsible, so too is Philemon to his household at Colossae.

Given the unique significance of the greeting that Paul communicates to Philemon through Epaphras, Epaphras too shares in Paul's social partnership of *koinōnia* and is a *koinōnos*. Epaphras' role in this *koinōnia* will be explained to the next generation of Jesus followers from Philemon's household in the letter to the Colossians. Epaphras' interpretation of Paul's greeting of *koinōnia* evident in Philemon and affirmed by Paul himself is expanded in the next generation, ensuring that the authoritative and discerning voice of Paul will continue to be heard and exert its influence, even though Paul has already died.

In summary, the letter's opening greeting formula is Paul's shorthand summary of his Gospel communicated throughout the letter and conveyed in Epaphras' closing greeting to Philemon and his household. Epaphras' "simple" greeting expresses Paul's desire that the Jesus followers at Colossae and in the Lycus Valley experience the depths of God's covenantal love and communion in their household, the wider Greco-Roman society of the valley, and the cosmos. Epaphras' greeting reveals how the conventional network and domestic relational patterns have moved to a new and more profound depth. It draws on the understanding of household and its inner pattern of relationship based on authority, friendship, and *koinōnia*, and reflective of the domestic pattern familiar to Paul's addressees.

Philemon's household membership is no longer limited to the conventional familial relationship that typified the Greco-Roman household. Membership now included other Jesus followers in the Lycus Valley and beyond. These other followers include members of *all* Jesus groups in Asia Minor, symbolized by Epaphras, Mark, Aristarchus, Demas, Luke, and their fictive kinship groups. The implicit power of Paul's greeting at the beginning of the letter, made explicit by Epaphras toward its end, now refocuses and redefines the domestic and social network of the Jesus assembly and its relationship in the Lycus Valley. This network reflects a more universal movement that will ultimately embrace the whole Greco-Roman world.

CHAPTER 4

Epaphras' Distinctiveness in Philemon

As noted in the previous chapter, Epaphras is distinguished from the rest of those sending greetings to Philemon by the authoritative nature of his greeting conveyed through Paul. He is also distinguished by his position in the list of greeters, as the first mentioned and by the designation Paul gives him. Paul describes him as "my fellow prisoner (*synaichmalōtos*) in Christ Jesus" (v. 23). The remaining four greeters (Mark, Aristarchus, Demas, and Luke) are given the title "my fellow workers" (*synergoi*, v. 24). These two designations are both similar and different. Clearly *synaichmalōtos* applies specifically to Epaphras, and we shall look at its significance shortly, especially in relationship to the only other place in his correspondence where Paul uses the same title. But the second description (*synergos*), which concludes the list of greeters, is frequently taken as applying only to Mark, Aristarchus, Demas, and Luke.

The final emphatic position in the sentence, however, arguably suggests a designation applicable to all who greet Philemon, including Epaphras. If this is the case, then Epaphras is foremost in Paul's retinue because of his specific relationship to Paul as "fellow prisoner in Christ Jesus" and, like Mark, Aristarchus, Demas, and Luke, as a "fellow worker." The same appelation, *synergos*, is also used by Paul of Philemon (v. 1). If *synergos* is the relationship Paul attributes to all those mentioned in the letter, the principal addressee (Philemon), and those who send their greetings, then it is also a title. *Synergos* reflects the common faith and bond in Jesus Christ they all share. This adds further weight to the rhetorical direction in which the letter moves.

Epaphras as Paul's "Fellow Worker" (*synergos*)

The Greek term *syn-ergos* indicates a collaborative relationship "with" (= *syn-*) Paul in his "work" (= *-ergos*) of proclaiming the Gospel of God and stabilizing in faith those who accept this Gospel. It is his favorite description for his collaborators (Rom 16:3, 9, 21; 1 Cor 3:9; 2 Cor 1:24; 6:1; 8:23; Phil 2:25; 1 Thess 3:2). A glance at the contexts in which the word occurs indicates that it includes women and men coworkers, cooperating with Paul in proclaiming the Gospel of God, especially in the cities and along the major trade routes where Paul found his focused audience, Israelites resident in cities with non-Israelite majorities. The expression implies a dynamic and active task-orientation focused on proclaiming the Gospel about the God of Israel who raised Jesus of Nazareth from the dead, making him Israel's messiah and cosmic Lord.[1] The *syn* also implies that those who work with Paul are likewise collaborating with God (as in 1 Cor 3:9). Their work is inspired by the presence of God energizing them in their preaching and accomplishing God's work, the absolute focus of Paul's ministry.[2] The divinely directed sense of *syn* becomes the essential component of communion between Paul and his collaborators. Its application to Philemon, the leader of a Jesus group household, and arguably, at the end of the letter, to Epaphras could also suggest that the role of *synergos* further entailed leadership in the Jesus group household, designating the primary leader in the household or the one to whom Paul imparted responsibility for the ongoing faith and worship of the household. The role of the *synergos* might also have included leadership at the table of the Lord in the Jesus group households. By the time Colossians was written, all these tasks, if only implicit in Philemon, were explicitly exercised by Epaphras.

Epaphras as Paul's "Fellow Prisoner" of War (*synaichmalōtos*)

Paul's first and most important description of Epaphras is as a *synaichmalōtos*. As we noted in our discussion of *synergos*, the *syn*- appendage to the main descriptor (*aichmalōtos*) accentuates the close bond Paul and Epaphras share. Their communion is based on faith in the Gospel of God, their commitment to Jesus, and their conviction that they are involved in the work of God. This communion and friendship parallel the relationship all the greeters have with Paul. However, Paul adds a further and significant feature in his relationship with Epaphras. It concerns their mutual imprisonment.

At the beginning of the letter Paul describes himself as a "prisoner of Christ Jesus," a designation he repeats again in verse 9. This suggests Paul's literal status as a prisoner. This is one of the factors that have led scholars to consider Philemon a "captivity letter." Paul has been incarcerated in Ephesus for proclaiming the Gospel of God. If the story in Acts 19 reflects the historical situation Paul experienced in his mission at Ephesus, and if he was imprisoned there (even though Acts mentions no imprisonment), his detention was the result of the social and economic upheaval his proclamation caused among the locals and those involved with the worship of Artemis.

The adjective *aichmalōtos* originally meant "prisoner of war" and in its verb form meant "to imprison." Its use as a verb, noun, or adjective is familiar in the New Testament (Luke 4:18; 21:24; Eph 4:8; 2 Tim 3:6; Rev 13:10), and Paul adopts it to describe the captivity that comes from sin (Rom 7:23) or the need to capture every thought to obey Christ (2 Cor 10:5). In this second sense *aichmalōtos* is the bond a person has with Jesus. In this way one committed to the Gospel becomes bound to Christ Jesus, the one "who has loved me, and given himself up for me" (Gal 2:20). Paul adopts and transfers this self-descriptor in his relationship to Jesus and his bond with Epaphras. Both have become enslaved to Jesus.

The explicit language of slavery Paul uses throughout his letters, and especially here, needs to be further nuanced, especially given the letter's context, the social institution of slavery and the master-slave relationship. Slavery pervaded Paul's world as an institution designed to obtain a labor force on behalf of elites. To this end the one enslaved is removed from the category of the human by the loss of freedom of decision and action.[3] Slavery was a form of social death and a "symbolic ritual of dishonor."[4] Slavery provided Paul with a "salvation metaphor" that could describe his relationship with Jesus.[5] His use of slavery language was not meant to accentuate a relationship of debasement, humiliation, or abusive treatment such as characterized masters' treatment of their slaves. Rather, the master-slave relationship accentuated God's lordship, revealed to human beings through Jesus, the kind of lordship and household protection offered to a slave in the house of the master. This description of "slavery" would also appeal to the slaves in Philemon's Colossian *ekklēsia*.

Slavery was the contradiction of freedom, for in slavery one is completely at the command and disposal of another.[6] Paul's use of the term and application to himself would reflect his devotion to Jesus, much like that of the devotees in an oriental religious cult who saw themselves as "slaves" of the god. Paul saw himself handed over to Christ, given up to his lordship and ready to obey his will. Paul's servitude as slave of Jesus was expressed in his stated desire to become a slave so that he could benefit many (1 Cor 9:19-23). His weakness, rather than being a source of failure, was a strength that would win over the weak to Christ.[7]

Drawing on imagery from the pervasive slave-master social institution, Paul could highlight, on the one hand, his inclusion in the Jesus group, which he experienced as a slave of Christ Jesus, and, on the other hand, the loyalty and fidelity to which he had committed himself in his relationship to Jesus. Paul had already asserted that Christ had brought freedom from the Torah and urged his addressees in Galatians 5:1: "do not submit again to a yoke of slavery." While Paul remained a person of his own time, and while we recognize the Greco-Roman institution of slavery as a social given, the relationship with God that emerges in Paul through Jesus begins to open up new ways of envisioning his world. Paul brings this vision to his letter to Philemon, and it carries through into Colossians.

Without urging explicit social reform concerning slavery, Paul realized that a new way of being and acting has come about through Christ. Those bonded to Jesus are no longer slaves, but sons and daughters of God (Gal 4:7) irrespective of gender and social status. Communion with Jesus removes any division between "slave and free" (Gal 3:28). In Jesus-group gatherings there is to be a kind of equality that transcends all social distinctions, though it does not remove or destroy them.[8] This is reflected in Paul's most explicit reflection about slavery within the community of Jesus followers in 1 Corinthians 7:20-24.

For Paul, too, his self-designation as a "slave" finds its biblical precedent in the Old Testament and its many references to "God's servants/slaves."[9] Paul is not merely imprisoned for his proclamation of the Gospel; he also belongs to the Lord Jesus. In this sense he is a "prisoner of Christ Jesus."

Epaphras as fellow prisoner "of war"

Paul also describes Epaphras not only as "my fellow prisoner" but as "my fellow prisoner *of war*." As noted above, Paul intends the designation figuratively, not in some literal sense as though Epaphras was actually arrested and imprisoned along with Paul or that he volunteered to share imprisonment with Paul.[10] If Paul had intended the expression to be taken more literally he would have used the well-known term associated with "being chained" (*dēsmios*) that occurs in Philemon 1 and 9.[11] At issue is not simply a physical imprisonment that has happened to Paul at Ephesus, from where he writes the letter to Philemon. Rather, the kind of imprisonment Paul means and sees in Epaphras is the common bond they share in Jesus. This is the Christ-oriented nature of their slavery implied in *synaichmalōtos*, not exclusively a status of literal enslavement, but above all loyalty and obedience in their explicit roles undertaken by command of their Lord Jesus.

The association of *aichmalōtos* (prisoner) with imprisonment as a result of *war* is unusual. More common Greek descriptors such as *syndedemenos* or *syndesmotes* were available to Paul to refer to his relationship with Epaphras based on a mutual experience of incarceration rather than as a result of war or conflict.[12] Paul refers to Epaphras as a "co-prisoner of war" at the end of the letter (v. 23) and himself as a "prisoner of Christ Jesus" at the beginning of the letter (v. 1). This creates an overarching frame and unifying theme in which the whole letter is set. Given their parallel and dominant placement in the letter, what can be inferred from one reference would, by association, apply to the other. What we can infer from Paul's reference at the beginning of the letter would apply equally to Epaphras. The common bond of imprisonment that Epaphras and Paul share is "of Christ Jesus" and has come about because of war.

The penal and military language of the letter drawn from imagery based on the ubiquity of the Roman army is not totally foreign in other genuine Pauline letters. Paul "serves as a soldier" (1 Cor 9:17) and "wages war for Christ" (2 Cor 10:3) in a task that is like a military "campaign" (1 Cor 10:4). These Pauline expressions might echo apocalyptic imagery of the great and ultimate cosmic battle that will usher in God's final judgment. This understanding, combined with the fact that in the letter to Philemon Paul calls himself "a prisoner of/for Christ Jesus" (vv. 1, 9), with Epaphras as "fellow prisoner of war" (v. 23), and names Archippus as a "fellow soldier" (v. 2), is highly suggestive of the social conflict in which Paul sees himself engaged along with Epaphras and Archippus. They are involved in a conflict with those who would thwart their divinely appointed mission to fellow Israelites, that is, those among them who reject the Gospel of God. What directs this conflict can be seen in the battle of cosmic and apocalyptic proportions waged by the forces opposed to Christ's cosmic rule as Lord.[13] After all, the Lord Jesus "after he has destroyed every ruler and every authority and power . . . must reign until he has put all his enemies under his feet" (1 Cor 15:24-25). This Pauline imagery will be further explored by the writer of the letter to the Colossians, where Epaphras will again appear and urge a battle against the elemental forces of the universe.

Furthermore, thought can finally be given to the phrase "in/ by Christ Jesus," which Paul links to the solidarity he and Epaphras share through their joint imprisonment. In Philemon v. 23, Epaphras is a "fellow prisoner *in* Christ Jesus." The Greek particle "in" could mean that Epaphras' solidarity with Paul is an experience of their union with Jesus. They are "in" him and no treatment, no matter how negative or violent, can cause them to become disassociated from Jesus. Their solidarity in faith is firmly established on the faithfulness of Jesus to his people, of which Paul and Epaphras are representative. The "in" could also be taken as instrumental: that is, Epaphras' imprisonment with Paul results from their activity on behalf of the Lord Jesus. In this sense they have been imprisoned with and by Jesus himself. This does not mean that Jesus' intention is that all those who are his disciples and proclaim the Gospel of God are intended to suffer or offer tragic witness. Rather, in everything that happens, even the experience of incarceration, God is involved through Jesus. He is instrumental in what occurs to those like Paul and Epaphras. The instrumental understanding of "in" then reaffirms the conviction revealed through Jesus of God's involvement in all human activity, even the most difficult of experiences.

Paul claims at the beginning of the letter the same kind of descriptor he uses for Epaphras toward the end, that he is a "prisoner *of* Christ Jesus" (v. 1). Just as the particle "in" in the phrase "in Christ Jesus" in reference to Epaphras in v. 23 is open to at least two interpretations, not mutually exclusive, Paul's use of the genitive ("*of* Christ Jesus") in reference to his imprisonment can also allow different yet complementary interpretations. The phrase can mean that Paul, like Epaphras, has been imprisoned *because of* Jesus as a result of his proclamation of the Gospel of God, or that Paul has been *claimed by* Jesus, or that Paul has allowed himself to be imprisoned *for the sake of* Jesus, that is, in order that he might be able to continue his task of proclaiming the Gospel concerning Jesus more transparently. All three interpretations are possible and perhaps intended.

Whatever final meaning we settle on regarding Epaphras' imprisonment "in Christ Jesus" (v. 23) and Paul's being prisoner "of Christ Jesus" (v. 1), both phrases emphasize the centrality of the Lord Jesus in their lives and mission, the sovereign claim, based on his lordship, that he has on them, and their recognition of Jesus in guiding and shaping their future ministry. Paul's reference to his imprisonment as a result of "Christ Jesus" emphasizes the *messianic* role of Jesus in Philemon's household, suggesting the household members' Israelite origins. After all, the title "messiah" is exclusively Israelite. These two aspects of the nature of Paul's relationship to Jesus are central. He is in relationship with "the Lord Jesus," a title that refers to Paul's real, living response to the person of Jesus. The "Christ" title would underscore the role of Jesus as God's faithful emissary to Israel and Israelites living in the Greco-Roman world of Paul and Epaphras.

In summary, more is implied by Paul's opening ascription to himself and the closing designation of Epaphras than first appears. He accentuates their common bond of faith, that they have been claimed ("imprisoned") by Jesus, who is the Lord; their lives and mission are shaped by and dependent on him and have resulted in their shared experience of physical detention. Finally, both references to the common experience of being a prisoner "of/in/by Christ Jesus" connect Paul and Epaphras. They occur at the beginning and toward the end of the letter. The relationship Paul and Epaphras share is centered on the Lord Jesus Christ; he is paramount to them; this key relationship acts as an overarching frame in which Paul's exhortation to Philemon is couched.

My interest in spelling out the inferences of the language Paul uses to describe Epaphras impinges on the social network strategy implied in the letter. The familiarity of language reflected through the terms "fellow worker" and "fellow prisoner of war" reflects Epaphras' status in the intimate network zone. But this relationship is not unique to Epaphras. It is into this zone that Philemon and his household are invited. The foundation for such familial intimacy is based on their relationship to Jesus Christ and their bond with him in *koinōnia*. This bond also alters the authoritative center of the domestic and social network. The letter began with Paul at the center of an ego-centered network. It concludes by implying Jesus as the real center of all the relational networks in which Philemon and his household are involved.

Before we conclude our study of Epaphras in Philemon there is a final aspect to *synaichmalōtos* worth highlighting. This adds

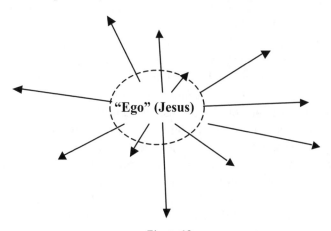

Figure 10
Recentering the Social Network

further weight to Epaphras' status and the importance he will assume in Colossians.

Synaichmalōtos *in Romans 16:7*

There is only one other place in Paul's genuine letters where the *synaichmalōtos* descriptor is found, and this is in the letter to the Romans, chapter 16. The term *synaichmalōtos* is applied to Andronicus and Junia (Rom 16:7).[14] Its occurrence here is rather significant and indicates that the title is to one of the highest and noblest descriptions Paul can offer any of his colleagues.

> Greet Andronicus and Junia, my relatives (*syngenēs*) and fellow prisoners (*synaichmalōtoi*) with me; they are out-standing among the apostles, and were before me in Christ. (Rom 16:7)

There are five things that we can note from Paul's reference to Andronicus and Junia. These have implications for our consideration of Epaphras.

First, Paul identifies them as "relatives" (*syngenēs*). This could mean that they are literally part of Paul's kinship group and thus "fellow Israelites" or, figuratively, close as members of his fictive kinship group, or both.[15] Whatever Paul's meaning here, it is clear that Andronicus and Junia, like Epaphras, belong to his intimate network zone. They would hold him in esteem and seek to ensure that his Gospel of God was faithfully represented.

Second, they are, like Epaphras, *synaichmalōtoi*. This may mean several things, all of them again not mutually exclusive. They may have shared imprisonment with Paul, undergone a time of imprisonment for their work of proclaiming the Gospel of God, or have become bonded (chained and imprisoned) to Jesus. Clearly, the relationship they have with Paul as *synaichmalōtoi* raises them, like Epaphras in the letter to Philemon, to a level of authority and prominence among Jesus followers. This status is further confirmed by the final two descriptors Paul gives them.

Third, they are called "outstanding among the apostles." This does not simply mean that they were highly regarded by the apostles themselves. From Romans 1:1 we know that Paul's use of apostle was distinctive and restrictive. The term "apostle" is a transliteration of the Greek word *apostolos*. It refers to "one sent" by another (Phil 2:25; 2 Cor 8:23) as a "change agent."[16] Paul's use restricts the title to those who constitute a distinct group of leaders within the Jesus groups. For Paul the title further designates those who have encountered the risen Jesus, have been commissioned by him to proclaim the Gospel, and, as agents of change, are responsible for the foundation and ongoing life of Jesus-group assemblies.[17]

Paul frequently begins his letters by calling himself an apostle (1 Cor 1:1; 2 Cor 1:1; Gal 1:1) or reflects on his call to apostleship in the middle of a fundamental argument (1 Cor 9:1-2; 15:9; 2 Cor 12:12). He applies the title to himself in Romans 1:1. Here he emphasizes his personal relationship and encounter with the risen Jesus, who has commissioned him to proclaim the Gospel to fellow Israelites living among the Gentiles (Rom 11:13). This encounter and commission are the basis for his firm conviction that he has "been set apart" (Rom 1:1) by Jesus and given authority to proclaim the Gospel about/from Jesus Christ. His personal introduction about his apostolic credentials in the opening greeting in Romans makes a claim to authority that confers credibility on what follows and grounds the authority of the letter in the resurrected Lord Jesus. If Paul's rich appreciation of "apostle" is transferred to Junia and Andronicus, then they probably belonged to a limited group of apostles appointed directly by the risen Jesus himself.[18] This appointment guaranteed them as authoritative representatives of the risen Jesus to the local households of Jesus followers at Ephesus, and perhaps they were responsible for its foundation or continuing life of faith. Their communion with Paul is forged more deeply because they too are apostles, though Paul recognizes himself as the "least of the apostles" (1 Cor 15:9) and "one untimely born" (1 Cor 15:8).

This claim of his apostolic status, which he reasserts at times against those who seek to discredit him, and the recognition of the belated nature of his apostolic call lead to Paul's fourth description of Andronicus and Junia. They are "before" him, that is, they are his seniors and have priority in their apostolic role.

Finally, Andronicus and Junia were "before" Paul "in Christ." This last phrase ("in Christ") connects naturally with Paul's recognition of the couple's chronologically senior apostolic status. Their being "in Christ" is the keystone of their apostleship. The positioning of the phrase is significant. It occurs at the end of the fourfold list of ascriptions Paul applies to the couple (*syngenēs*, *synaichmalōtoi*, "outstanding among the apostles," "before me"). Its immediate and primary link is to their apostolic priority over Paul. Further, "in Christ" becomes the overarching context that deepens and explains the meaning of all the qualities Paul recognizes in the couple. Their priority is not because of age, but of the length of time they have been apostles "in Christ." Their commission occurred before Paul was appointed by the risen Jesus as an apostle.

This study of the language in Romans 16:7 with Paul's description of Andronicus and Junia is helpful as we appreciate Paul's reference to Epaphras in Philemon. The apostolic status of Andronicus and Junia is linked with their being "fellow prisoners of war" (*synaichmalōtoi*) "in Christ." While the "in Christ" expression is frequent throughout Paul's genuine letters, the *synaichmalōtos* term is only found in two places, here in Romans 16 and in association with Epaphras in the letter to Philemon. In other words, though Epaphras is not an apostle like Paul, Andronicus, and Junia, he is firmly linked to all three through the shared experience of being *synaichmalōtos*. While this does not equate to being an apostle, it draws him into the common experience of those whom Paul considers apostles in Rome's Jesus-group households. This association reflects a common experience with Andronicus and Junia that no other companion or colleague had, as well as the esteem in which Paul holds Epaphras, the authority he has by association with two of the Roman apostles, and the high regard that Philemon and his faith community would have for him.

Summary

Let me summarize what we learn about Epaphras in Paul's letter to Philemon.

The singular description of Epaphras in one of Paul's last letters is rich and revealing. The language Paul uses of Epaphras indicates his colleagueship with Paul in his activity as well as their common relationship to Jesus, to whom they are bonded. Epaphras is further endorsed as the primary greeter to Philemon and his Jesus-group household and authorized to explicate Paul's graceful blessing at the letter's beginning and conclusion.

The place where these descriptors appear in the letter, how they link up with similar expressions found in Paul's other letters, and the manner of their application to Paul's other companions—all these help us come to an appreciation of Paul's regard for Epaphras. Paul's description of Epaphras as a *koinōnos* ("companion in faith"), a *synergos* ("coworker"), a *synaichmalōtos* ("fellow prisoner of war") "in Christ Jesus" attests to Epaphras' authority and status in the eyes of Philemon and his Jesus household and the role he has already played. It reveals the esteem in which he is held by Paul and lays the foundation for the role he will later play among Jesus followers in the Lycus Valley. Paul likewise associates *synaichmalōtos* with Andronicus and Junia in Romans 16:7, describing them as apostles. Paul's application of this term to Epaphras raises his authority at least implicitly to quasi-apostolic status. We shall shortly see how this authority will be explicitly recognized in the letter to the Colossians.

Epaphras' description is set against the backdrop of the conventional network and domestic patterns of the Greco-Roman world presumed and implied in the letter. While Paul assumes the center of the ego-patterned network at the beginning of his address to Philemon, this network and its domestic context are reinterpreted in light of the central relationship to the Lord Jesus. A shift occurs in the network relationship between Paul and the letter's addressees and greeters. They move into Paul's intimate network zone, which reconfigures the pattern of their domestic relationships focused in *koinōnia* on the Lord Jesus. He, and not Paul, is now the heart of the ego-centered network.

The earlier analysis of social network and the patron-client relation that preceded our study of Philemon also shows other differences. These emerge out of the focus on Jesus in the reconstituted ego-centered network and the development of a domestic network pattern along fictive kinship lines. In this newly emerging domestic configuration the network pattern is more symmetrical, with its participants linked by friendship and *koinōnia* and enjoined to adopt a spirit of inclusivity rather than hierarchy.

CHAPTER FIVE

Epaphras in the Letter to the Colossians

While there is only one reference to Epaphras in Paul's genuine letters (Phlm 23), Colossians offers us two (Col 1:7; 4:13). Their context and position in the letter's overall development reveal the leadership and authority Epaphras has assumed at Colossae at a time when new circumstances and issues had arisen since Paul's death. The writer "summons" Paul from the grave to speak freshly to Jesus-group households and to affirm their leadership.[1] The Pauline writer also seeks to validate the authority of Paul's coworkers and their ability to address this new social situation authentically in his name. In this context Epaphras receives special attention that is consistent with and expands upon the way he was presented by Paul in Philemon. The writer endorses Epaphras as Paul's legitimate agent and founder of the Jesus group at Colossae.

To appreciate the uniqueness of Epaphras' role among the Colossians, we must first get a sense of the writer's concerns. This provides us with a vantage point to assess the role played by Epaphras as a member of Paul's network and the kind of network he seeks to establish among the Colossian Jesus group.

The Colossian Concerns

On a first reading of Colossians it is clear that the writer's interests are very different from Paul's in his letter to Philemon. The writer is interested in responding to local religious and philosophical concerns that seem attractive to the letter's audience and influence their religious practice. These emerge in the body of the letter in chapter 2. In 2:4 the writer wants to protect the Colossians from being deluded "by plausible arguments." In 2:8 and 2:16-23 the nature of such "arguments" becomes explicit:

> See that no one captures you through philosophy and empty deception according to the traditions of human beings, according to the elemental spirits of the cosmos and not according to Christ. (2:8)
>
> Therefore do not let anyone judge you in food and drink or in observing festivals, new moons, or sabbaths. These are only a shadow of what is to come, but the body is of Christ.[2] Let no one disqualify you, insisting on false humility and worship of angels, relying on visions, being vainly conceited by a human way of thinking, and not holding fast to the head, from whom every body, by means of ligaments and sinews, is nurtured, being held together to grow the growth that is of God. If you have died with Christ to the elemental spirits of the cosmos, why do you live ruled by the cosmos? "Do not handle, Do not taste, Do not touch"? All these refer to things that perish with use, according to the rules and teachings of human beings. These have an appearance of wisdom through self-imposed piety, false humility, and severe bodily discipline, but they have value only in satisfying self-indulgence. (2:16-23)

The issues that concern the writer emerge clearly from these two passages. While interests focused on the Lord Jesus pervade the writer's agenda, here the main concerns are about rituals, beliefs, and practices.[3] Some Colossians seem to be influenced by a philosophy that is regarded by the writer as an inauthentic human way of thinking ("empty deception according to the traditions of human beings"—2:8), that emphasizes the role of nonhuman forces and powers ("elemental spirits of the universe"—2:8, 20) that seek to entrap people. These Colossians form a network pattern with its own rituals, structures, and alliances that is in conflict with the Pauline fictive kinship pattern of partnership relationships grounded in Christ through baptism. As we shall see, Paul's network is enunciated in Colossians 1. The "alternative network," on the other hand, is influenced by a local cosmology in which the elemental spirits hold sway and need to be assuaged. These nonhuman personal forces could well be identified with celestial "powers" and principalities and somehow linked to "the worship of angels" (2:18), arguably an Israelite cult focused on angels.[4] The nodes of alignment of this alternative celestial network in the diagram below, though not comprehensive, illustrate the complexity of relationships.

Whatever the nature of the angelic worship, the celestial network pattern reflects the writer's concern about the visionary, ecstatic nature of a physical system of asceticism promoted by the writer's opponents. Reliance on these human regulations and a multifaceted ascetical regime rather than on the heart of the Gospel—the resurrected Lord Jesus Christ—has compromised the faithfulness of the Colossian Jesus followers.[5] They

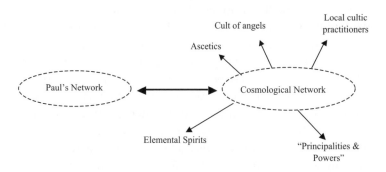

Figure 11
Paul's Network and Alternative Cosmological Network

seek to submit to a heavenly network apparently ruled by elemental spirits and angels with whom the Colossians need har-
monious relationships. Only in this way, it is argued, through
rigorous asceticism and what appears to be an almost proto-
Gnostic denunciation of the physical world, Israelite in inspiration, will they be able to ward off social evil and have access to
the divine fullness.[6] Subservience, voluntary submission to the
celestial and angelic powers is the sure guarantee for participa-
tion in divine life. In this philosophical way of life there is no
room for the Lord Jesus Christ, or if the Lord Jesus is central,
submission to regulations has become more important than the
resurrected Jesus.[7] Alternatively, access to angels is proposed as
much easier than access to God. The worship of angels becomes
the divine substitute.[8]

The Colossian Writer's Approach

A delicate balance needs to be struck by the writer of the letter.
On the one hand there is a truth in the position of those who
seem to be offering an erroneous way of life. This truth concerns
their appreciation of the spirit world, the acknowledgment of
human involvement in respect for celestial powers, and the importance of an angelic cosmology. But the writer interprets their
emphasis as one that leads the Colossians away from the fundamental social faith network in Christ involving local Jesus-
group households and their appreciation of the ritual initiation
into Christ's life through baptism. In the writer's view, as Colossian followers of Jesus seek a path toward divine communion
they seem to combine authentic Gospel insights with practices
found in the worship forms of local Judeo-Greco-Roman reli-
gions and Phrygian cults. They "seem," because the exact nature
of the syncretistic practice is unclear. Its hypothetical reconstruction suggested above is only possible through reading behind
the text of Colossians and trying to reconstruct the various network patterns. The variety of these networks would be further

expressed in the Phrygian and Anatolian folk traditions, local Israelite beliefs about angels, and other cultic practices.[9] Besides the Pauline domestic network, the cosmological network, deriving from local folk traditions, adds another layer of network patterns that influences the Colossian Jesus group and contributes to the "infinite" and "total" network described earlier.

The Colossian opponents should not be thought of as a single, identifiable syncretistic group, but rather as a number of people who exhibit a variety of philosophical and ascetical tendencies shared across a network of religious groups.[10] These tendencies might have been adopted by Jesus teachers and absorbed by some Colossians into their way of living and doctrinal thinking. The rigorous ascetical conduct of some would have influenced their relational network pattern.

This discussion about the nature of ingroup concerns and the complexity of network patterns affecting the people addressed in the letter provides the context for considering the role Epaphras plays among the Colossians. Making this role explicit is central to the writer's agenda. Though the Colossians are now

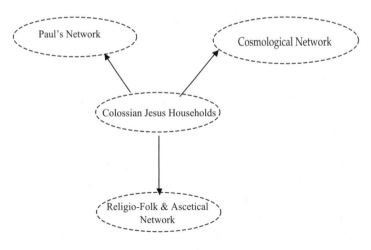

Figure 12
Relational Network Patterns in Colossae

without the benefit of the wisdom of the historical Paul, they are not deprived of his teaching communicated through Epaphras. The writer's reference to Epaphras would be critical in steering the Colossians back to authentic Pauline perspectives. As we shall now see, Epaphras' authority is important to counterbalance the religious knowledge and experience offered by the philosophy of the letter's opponents, who are in need of mature wisdom and appropriate discernment.

The Opening Greeting (Colossians 1:1-2)

The ego-centered network is established in the letter's opening verses and parallels the pattern noted in Philemon. The letter begins with the standard Pauline greeting (1:1). It refers to the senders of the letter, Paul and Timothy, and the addressees. Paul is the center. Timothy shares in Paul's authority as "brother" and belongs to Paul's intimate network zone. The addressees are mentioned with the standard Pauline blessing. The familial language of the domestic Jesus-group network reflects the fictive kinship relationship already familiar to us from Philemon.

> Paul, an apostle of Christ Jesus, through the will of God, and Timothy, brother.
>
> To the saints in Colossae and faithful brothers and sisters in Christ.
>
> Grace to you and peace from God our Father. (Col 1:1-2)

From the outset the writer affirms the fidelity and ingroup orientation of the letter's audience. They are in communion with each other and the writer because they are "in Christ"—an expression already familiar from Philemon. In the letter to the Colossians "in Christ" takes on added significance, given the particular issue the writer will seek to address. How to be "in Christ" will be the focus of the writer's concern, especially in reference to the addressees' incorporation "in Christ" through baptism. The salutation concludes (1:2) with a blessing of "grace"

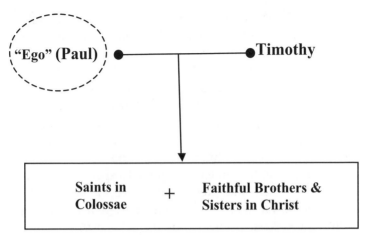

Figure 13
The Intimate Network Zone in Colossians 1

and "peace," a formula already discussed in reference to Phile-mon. This blessing is indicative of the intimate network zone in which greeters and addressees share and the divine blessing that comes from such intimacy.

The next section of the letter mirrors the thanksgiving section typical of Paul's genuine letters. These opening verses praise the faith life of the Colossians and the role Epaphras has played in enabling them to come to such faith. They celebrate the addressees' faith, love, and active response to the Gospel, all the fruit of good instruction (1:6b-7a). This leads to the first mention of Epaphras and the recognition of his activity as proclaimer and interpreter of the Gospel of God (1:7-8). Everything that leads to 1:7 with its explicit mention of Epaphras reveals the content and method of his instruction (1:3-6) and his role in assuring the Colossians' fidelity to the Pauline tradition.

Epaphras as "Faith Educator" and Colleague in Paul's Network

There are two further features that make the thanksgiving segment of the letter significant. First, it tells how the Colossian followers of Jesus learned the Gospel of God. Second, this allows us to view in one early Jesus group the practice of what might be called, albeit anachronistically, faith education, of which Epaphras was the principal practitioner. By "faith education" I mean that the letter writer was concerned with the formation of Jesus-group members in the way of life that flowed from the proclamation of the Gospel of God. This entailed the ability to discern authentic truth and to recognize and affirm the place of genuine religious experience within that discernment. The writer was concerned about the authenticity of the Gospel of God as proclaimed by Paul and interpreted for the Colossians by Epaphras, and about the role religious experience played in validating the truth of this Gospel. In other words, the writer of Colossians was especially concerned about forming local Jesus followers in a way of living deriving from Paul's appreciation of the Lord Jesus and the activity of God. This is what Epaphras proclaimed to them and interpreted for them while he affirmed the centrality of religious interiority, experience, and enlightenment in the growth of faith. These were necessary elements connected to deepening the Colossians' appreciation of their inherited faith tradition.[11] Epaphras helped the writer formulate an approach to the truth about Jesus sensitive to the religious dimensions of human experience. The Pauline writer regarded Epaphras' role as remarkable and affirmed this in the opening section of the letter.

The explicit mention of Epaphras and his strategic location in the letter's opening thanksgiving highlight his place in Paul's network and his role in the wider familial network of the Jesus assembly at Colossae. His mention thus expands the original pattern observed in the letter's opening verses, placing Epaphras alongside Timothy in sharing Paul's authority and intimate network zone, and centering him, like "Paul" and Timothy, in the Colossian network pattern related to "the saints in Colossae" and the "faithful brothers and sisters in Christ."

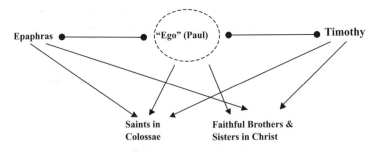

Figure 14
Epaphras within the Network

Epaphras' Qualities (Colossians 1:7-8)

The way the writer positions Epaphras in the rhetorical development of the thanksgiving also links Epaphras' activity as instructor to what follows in the letter and the vision the writer offers its audience. Epaphras becomes a bridge between what *has been* (the Pauline tradition revealed in the four verses of the thanksgiving, 1:3-6), what *is* (the controversy with opponents that is yet to be disclosed), and what *will be* (the writer's cosmic Christology and its implication for the ongoing life of the Colossian Jesus groups).[12] All this is clear from the explicit description the writer gives of Epaphras in 1:7-8. What the Colossians have learned leads to his description. They have

> learned from Epaphras
> our beloved fellow slave
> who is a faithful minister of Christ
> on your/our behalf
> and indeed has declared to us
> your love in the Spirit. (Col 1:7-8)

The writer presents Epaphras first as the primary proclaimer of the Gospel to the Colossians and their instructor in Gospel ways as well. The statement here indicates that Epaphras, not

Paul, was remembered as founder of the Jesus group at Colossae. Since Paul insisted that he does not "build on another man's foundation" (Rom 15:20), the posthumous Paul of this letter to the Colossians writes in the same spirit revealed in the letter to the Romans, that is, to fellow Jesus-group members whom he did not recruit. It was Epaphras who proclaimed the Gospel of God at Colossae and instructed first believers in the new way of thinking and acting. Instructional language ("learned") is explicit. The nature of what he taught and his method of forming them "in Christ" are described in 1:3-6, which we shall look at later. As the one who proclaimed the Gospel at Colossae, Epaphras is the founder of the Jesus group there. As instructor, he is the one around whom they gathered to reflect on the implications of the Gospel in their Jesus-group households. The language of instruction the writer uses in verse 7 is also associated in the Gospel narratives with discipleship. From this point of view Epaphras' teaching role has deepened the spirit of discipleship among the Colossians.

Epaphras as Paul's "beloved fellow slave" (Colossians 1:7b)

Epaphras is also described as "our beloved fellow slave." As we have already noted relative to the letter to Philemon, Paul uses "slave" terms, even explicitly describing himself as a slave (in Rom 1:1; Gal 1:10; Phil 1:1). Epaphras' description in Col 1:7 as Paul's "fellow slave" emphasizes the depth of their relationship. The spirit of partnership Epaphras had with Paul, reflected in the letter to Philemon, continues here in Colossians and is emphatic. They have shared imprisonment together and now the writer furthers the Pauline memory of Epaphras by describing him as one who shares with Paul the status of slave. Given Epaphras' role at Colossae, this description of both as fellow slaves allows the Colossians to welcome Paul's teaching with credibility.[13]

Later the Colossian writer will specifically address slaves in their relationships to others in the household, especially their masters (3:22–4:1). The letter's instruction to slaves will have special appeal, given their shared status with Epaphras and Paul as "fellow slaves" and the possibility of Epaphras' original servile status before embarking on this new role in the Jesus movement. Their mutual slavery, as a metaphor for their commitment, loyalty, and obedience to Jesus, and Epaphras' servile background would further their solidarity with all slaves and freedmen and -women.

The writer's instructions to slaves occur in the context of what is called a "household code of conduct." This sort of household code was familiar in the Greek world of civilized persons (that is what "Greek" meant), since it expressed conventional wisdom to preserve order and security in the household and the wider social unit to which the household was attached. The writer's intention in citing the code in its reworked formula was to help cement the Colossian Jesus household as an integral part of the wider community. These Jesus householders were encouraged through the code to live exemplary lives and model the best social virtues. This might explain the code's emphasis on "ruling and being ruled" in the three household pairs: wives-husbands, children-parents, and masters-slaves. The longest part of the household instruction concerns slaves and their relationship to their masters. In this instruction in Colossians 3:22-23 we gain deeper insights into how the writer understood Paul and Epaphras as "fellow slaves."

The Slaves of the Colossian Jesus Households

Some scholars have suggested that the lengthy exhortation to slaves was in response to a problem that was occurring among the Colossians.[14] This, they argue, might have been due to the social unrest created by slaves seeking their freedom as envisioned in Galatians 3:28. As a result of this Pauline teaching, slaves who were followers of Jesus might have considered themselves no longer slaves in the Jesus household because of their emancipation brought about by Christ. But rather than as a social correction to the quest for physical freedom by slaves, perhaps a more likely context for the Colossian writer's appeal to the household code and address to slaves might be found in Paul's teaching in 1 Corinthians 7:21-24.

> Were you a slave when called? Do not be concerned about it. Even if you can gain your freedom, make use of your present condition now more than ever. For whoever was called in the Lord as a slave is a freed person belonging to the Lord, just as whoever was free when called is a slave of Christ. You were bought with a price; do not become slaves of human masters. In whatever condition you were called, brothers and sisters, there remain with God.

This passage reflects Paul's attitude of accommodation to the social practice of institutionalized manumission. While welcoming manumission and its accompanying status recognition of freedom for slaves, Paul follows contemporary social practice (called *paramonē*) and considers that freed slaves still remained linked in service and loyalty to their former masters. Paul's emphasis in his advice in 1 Corinthians 7 is valid whether it applied to someone who was still a slave or free. In either case their primary relationship was their union with the Lord Jesus Christ. A person who was a slave would always be free in relationship to Jesus (1 Cor 7:22a); someone free would always be "a slave of Christ"—bound by a union with him (1 Cor 7:22b). Whatever social state Jesus' followers lived in, they would always "remain with God" (1 Cor 7:24). This all-embracing fundamental relationship, in which one "remained," offered the kind of vision Paul thought should govern and guide all the familiar social and household networks of his day.

The balance Paul tried to communicate in 1 Corinthians 7:21-24 later filters through the instruction to slaves found in the Colossian household code. It guides the way the writer instructs slaves committed to Jesus in relationship to their masters. Their owners are encouraged to grant manumission as a reward to obedient and faithful slaves, though manumission was not considered automatic.[15] The writer reinforces the social expectation that slaves were required to be obedient to their household masters. This emphasis on the slave's obedience helps to buttress the impression that Jesus households were places of social cohesion that encouraged a considerable degree of latitude among slaves. The more important problem with regard to the Colossian slaves was not their manumission, but the false teaching to which they would have been exposed from the writer's opponents.[16] The writer critiques the apparent emphasis of the letter's adversaries on the importance of earthly "fleshly" markers that would guarantee their heavenly future (Col 2:8-23). These opponents seem to stress the value of external structures and observable indicators that offer a tangible sense of community and identity. This has occurred at a time of transition from "anti-structured liminality back to social structure."[17] That context would move the writer to stress baptism as the only necessary ritual that creates identity in Christ, rather than the kinds of rituals and ascetic practices proposed by the opponents. Relationship to Christ is more important than anything. For this reason, slaves are encouraged to

> obey in everything your masters according to the flesh, not with eye-service as people pleasers, but with simplicity of heart, fearing the Lord. Whatever you do, put your whole selves into it, as for the Lord and not for human beings, knowing that from the Lord you will receive the reward of the inheritance. It is the Lord Christ you serve. (Col 3:22-24)

The writer's stress on a slave's relationship to Christ becomes important in responding to the false teaching about ascetic practices to which they have been exposed. That slaves are addressed directly in this instruction means that they are obviously actual members of the Jesus groups of Colossae. It affirms the appropriateness of Epaphras' introduction as Paul's "fellow slave." They are asked to obey their masters "according to the flesh." This establishes the context and limitation of their obedience.

They are to obey them as earthly masters, and it is in the sphere of the ordinary and menial that they are to maintain their relationship. This duty is to be continuously exercised as an authentic expression of themselves and not only while they are being scrutinized by their masters or for appearance's sake (v. 22b). They are to be wholehearted and single-minded in their commitment to their duty to their masters, who are reminded in turn that *their* master is God (4:1).

God's supremacy over the household head qualifies the authority that masters, as followers of Jesus and conscious of God's presence and authority, are to exercise over their slaves.[18] In this setting slaves are to conduct themselves as "fearing the Lord" (v. 22c). Their relationship in the earthly household is located within the more important relationship with God characterized as respectful ("fearing"). This relationship is the overarching context within which all household activities occur and that all members are encouraged to remember. This understanding leads to verse 23: "Whatever you do, put your whole selves into it, as for the Lord and not for human beings." This reinforces the christological foundation for the slaves' conduct, that what is done is "for the Lord" rather than for human beings. This conviction lays the foundation for real emancipation, by which slaves enjoy true freedom, an idea that is summed up in verse 24: "It is the Lord Christ you serve." God is the source of any reward, even emancipation, and the slave's service to the master is, in reality, service to Jesus Christ.

All these reflections about slavery based on Colossians 3:22-24 apply equally to the way Epaphras and Paul are considered "fellow slaves." Their relationship is fundamentally to God through their obedience to Jesus Christ. God will reward them; through him they are able to exercise their servitude in the Jesus-group household. This relationship with God is also the reason why the writer appends the adjective "beloved" to Epaphras' slave status (1:7b). It specifies his relationship with Paul, and through Paul to the Colossian community; being "beloved" also reveals the divine source of Epaphras' mission and status.

As Paul's "beloved," Epaphras is his legitimate spokesman and interpreter. Their partnership in faith, reinforced through their shared slave status, makes Epaphras "beloved." It is the fruit of a communal life lived in union with Jesus and their sharing of the Gospel of God. This communal sharing is now no longer physical. They are not in the same physical location; their shared attachment transcends place and time.

Epaphras as Paul's "faithful minister of Christ" (Colossians 1:7c)

The writer next describes Epaphras as "faithful minister of Christ," a coherent expansion of his role in light of the slave discussion above. The reference point for all servitude here is the Lord Jesus Christ, as we have already noted. This idea will occur later in the letter when the writer describes the slave's total dedication as owed to God through Jesus Christ rather than to an earthly master. That relationship is established here in reference to Epaphras, now described as a "faithful minister" of Christ. Epaphras' activity as instructor reflects his relationship to Jesus and is the source of ministerial fidelity. The English translation "minister" is the Greek word *diakonos,* which in the Pastoral Letters of the late first and early second century CE becomes a publicly designated role within the Jesus groups. The classical understanding of *diakonos* in Hellenistic society was of one who acted as a messenger or diplomat on behalf of a person of higher social standing.[19] This would make Epaphras the authorized agent or representative of Jesus Christ, endorsed and supported by Paul.[20] The agent duties Epaphras performs are "of Christ." This means that Jesus is both the source of Epaphras' instructional activity (in the sense of "from Christ") and its focus ("about Christ"). This explicit focus on the Lord Jesus further validates Epaphras' presidential and educative role among the Colossians.

To Epaphras' description as a faithful servant the writer adds a further phrase to complement and expand the meaning of his role. This concerns those on whose behalf Epaphras acts. There is a problem at this point in the Greek manuscripts that makes it hard to decide on the authorizing agency for Epaphras' activity. Manuscripts are equally divided over whether Epaphras acts on behalf of "you," that is, on behalf of the Colossians, or on "our" behalf, that is on behalf of Paul (and Timothy).[21] The second possibility is favored by many commentators and seems most consistent with Epaphras' presentation to the Colossians as Paul's authoritative interpreter. If this is correct and Epaphras acts "on our behalf," then he is Paul's authorized representative. Through Epaphras, Paul speaks, teaches, refutes, and encourages. Epaphras enables Paul to speak from the grave and close the chronological gap between past and present. This is particularly pertinent given the deutero-Pauline nature of the letter and the need for its writer to mediate Paul's authority. The writer's double use of the plural in 1:7 ("*our* fellow slaves" and "on *our* behalf") reinforces the communal nature and focus of Epaphras' ministerial agency. This "our" recognizes that Epaphras serves in solidarity with the Pauline tradition, infused with Paul's liberating spirit and informed by his theological vision.

Epaphras as Agent between the Colossians and Paul

Colossians 1:8 adds another dimension to Epaphras' agency that also involves "Paul." Epaphras is described as letting Paul know of the Colossian situation and the faith lives of the Jesus-group households. The writer will expand on this in the final phrase of the verse, "your love in the Spirit." Epaphras' activity of reporting concerns his clarification and explanation of the situation. This is more than a simple act of reporting; it involves interpretation. What the Pauline writer "hears" from Epaphras as mentioned in 1:4 provides a link back to the beginning of the thanksgiving section of the letter. The reference to what "Paul" hears (presumably from Epaphras) in 1:4 and what he informs him about in 1:8 means that Epaphras is a conduit. He connects the Colossian community back to the authentic teaching and witnessing spirit of the historical Paul. From Paul's "hearing" of Epaphras (1:4) and the information supplied to him (1:8) emerges credible instruction in harmony with Paul's original vision about Jesus kept alive by his colleagues, collaborators, and "fellow slaves." Among these, Epaphras is most esteemed in the eyes of the Colossian community. Epaphras' act of interpretation, of informing "Paul," takes on special significance in light of the absence of the historical Paul.

This "informing" of Paul is, in fact, an act of dialogue and reflective meditation on the present situation in light of the Gospel as proclaimed by Paul and witnessed in Epaphras' activity. Epaphras is not only Paul's mouthpiece on whose behalf he acts. He also represents Paul's heart—the fruit of meditation and reflective contemplation from which action results. The shift in the letter from an ego-centered network focused on Paul to one that now focuses on the Lord Jesus means that Epaphras also represents Jesus' heart, the fruit of meditation on the role of the resurrected Jesus.

The final phrase of 1:8 reveals the central nature of Epaphras' information to Paul and the focus of Epaphras' reflection to which his proclamation and instruction respond. It concerns "your love in the Spirit." "Spirit" could mean the human spirit, and the phrase might refer to the spirit of mutual attachment shared among the Colossians. But it is more likely that the writer's reference is to God's Spirit. As we have seen in our reflection on Epaphras as Paul's fellow slave and as "faithful minister," the writer's orientation naturally led to a consideration of the centrality of God in the Pauline project. This orientation to God would have come from Paul's experience of the risen Jesus and been expressed through his instructions, especially to Epaphras, first as a convert to the Gospel of God, later as Paul's ministerial colleague, and now as Paul's representative to the Colossians. God's Spirit has energized and empowered the Colossians and is the source of the group attachment tangibly expressed within the Colossian Jesus-group households. This manner of life based on mutual attachment through God's Spirit is the focus of Epaphras' information to Paul. It is the basis for Epaphras' interpretation reflected upon in the light of Paul's spirit that resources the teaching to which the writer bears witness.

Content and Method of Epaphras' Teaching

With Epaphras' identity and authority confirmed in 1:7-8, the writer moves to explore the implications of Epaphras' way of teaching. This exploration firmly grounds the addressees in a renewed appreciation of the risen and cosmic Christ and responds to some of the concerns raised by the writer's opponents. Before we briefly consider this it is important to identify the content, nature, and method of teaching associated with Epaphras and revealed in Col 1:3-6. Here in compressed form is the essence of Epaphras' teaching from which the Colossians have "learned" (1:7) and on which the rest of the letter builds, faithful to Paul's teaching as communicated through his authorized spokesperson, Epaphras.

As the thanksgiving begins (1:3) the writer thanks God in prayer for the Colossians. Then in a series of connected phrases the Pauline writer unpacks the reason for thanking God. It is based on what "Paul" has heard from Epaphras as the community conduit and interpreter about Jesus Christ.

As theological interpreter Epaphras acts to aid the Colossian Jesus households in reflecting on their present situation. The letter to the Colossians is the fruit of Epaphras' reflection on the activity of God revealed in God's raising Jesus from the dead. Working from the premise that Paul is not the writer of the letter and that a number of terms that occur in Colossians are not present in the authentic Pauline writings, we note that Epaphras has contributed to Paul's teaching. He is, then, more than a "conduit." His success as Paul's interpreter and educator about the outcome of God's raising Jesus is demonstrated by the way his insights concerning Jesus have been incorporated into the letter by himself (if he is its writer) or another. In the opening chapter these insights concern the Colossians' faith in the God who raised Jesus from the dead (1:4), which is demonstrated in the reality of their mutual attachment displayed in their assemblies. The way of living rooted in this faith in God is seen as the tangible expression of the hope reserved especially for them by God, about which they have heard "by the word of truth of the gospel" (1:5b). Much hinges on how this rich and complex phrase "by the word of truth of the gospel" is interpreted.

"Truth"

"By" translates the Greek *en*, which, as we have seen in reference to "in Christ," can be understood in different ways that are not mutually exclusive. *En* is either spatial ("in the word"), instrumental ("through the word"), or temporal ("when the word . . .").[22] The "word" is the proclamation and instruction the Colossians have heard from Epaphras. The "truth" of the proclaimed word, which is identified as "the gospel," raises a central issue and theme that the writer's opponents contest—in what and where truth about God is to be found.

In 1:5b we find the first of two summaries about the essential content of Epaphras' teaching among the Colossians. His teaching is summarized as "the word of truth of the gospel." His teaching is the source of the tradition the writer explores in counteracting the false teaching experienced by the Colossians. His word is also effective; the writer describes it as "bearing fruit" and "growing among" them and throughout the whole world (1:6). This word, "heard" and "understood," is the fruit of Epaphras' educational activity. In 1:7b the Pauline writer offers a second summary of Epaphras' teaching: the Colossians "have heard and come to know the grace of God in truth." This second summary echoes the "word of truth of the gospel" of verse 5b and expands on it. There are three points to note about these summaries.

First, the summaries explicate the educational dynamic in which the Colossians are involved. They are engaged experientially with Epaphras' teaching; they "have heard." This listening posture is more than a passive reception of what is taught. It involves a total engagement of receptivity, reflection, and integration. This leads the Colossians to "know" and comprehend the truth of what they have been taught. They have come to "knowledge." To "know" also implies a certain intimacy and familiarity that permeates their lives, guides them, and leads to behavioral outcomes. They learn to experience, and thus "know."

Second, through Epaphras the Colossians have encountered God's "grace" (*charis*). The Greek word *charis* is translated *gratia* in Latin. In English the best translation is "favor," although it is often translated "grace," a sort of transliteration from Latin. In first-century Mediterranean society favor referred to something, either not available at all or not available now, that one seeks from a patron in order to deal with some problem. "Favor" is a term proper to the patron-client system described above. What clients want and need of patrons are favors of one sort or another, and what patrons need from clients are recognition and acknowledgment of the patrons' honor and claim to worth.

In the theological analogy according to which God is looked upon as a patron, what God dispenses are favors. The term "favor" (or "grace") is thus filled with theological depth especially in the story of Jesus, who considers God as Father (that is, Patron). Starting from Jesus, the image of God as Patron is built upon within the Pauline tradition, as we saw in the greetings in Philemon and Colossians. In Paul's letters the greeting became the means by which God's patronage is remembered and revealed as present among those whom Paul addressed—a point we have already reflected upon in reference to the greetings Paul and Epaphras send to Philemon. "Grace" for Paul is God's favor revealed through God's raising Jesus from the dead. It is expressed in that uniquely Pauline expression, "justification," meaning effective divine approval. This background is present in the writer's reference to God's "grace in truth." Epaphras' proclamation has allowed the Colossians to experience the loving-kindness of God's presence, revealed by God in the experience of the Lord Jesus and, as the writer will explore, confirmed in baptism.

Third, the teaching, as God's grace/favor, comes to the Colossians "in (*en*) truth" through Epaphras. The variety of ways of translating *en* indicates that this truth can, like the "word" (*logos*) in verse 5b, be spatial ("in the truth") as pervading their experience totally; it can be instrumental ("through the truth") as the cause of their conviction about their encounter with God's grace; or it can be temporal ("when the truth . . ."), allowing for the truth of the encounter with God's grace to become known over time and through their history. The repetition of "truth" in the two summaries alerts us to its importance in the letter. This has implications for the way Christ is appreciated or regarded by the Colossians, which is unpacked in the magnificently rich christological hymn of 1:15-18 with its extended commentary in 1:19-20.[23]

Epaphras has faithfully instructed the Colossians in this truth, we learn in 1:6, through an interpersonal dynamic ("hearing") that has engaged them in the depths of their being. The writer's use of language and the complexity of the sentence structure reflect the seriousness of what is at stake here. The two aspects of the Gospel's "truth" and what the Colossians "have come to know" (i.e., experiential knowledge) are linked and become echoed in the later writings, 1 and 2 Timothy and Titus.[24] But here in Colossians they have a unique nuance. At stake are the meaning of salvation, the credibility of the Gospel, and the authenticity of the community's teaching.

The expression "truth of the Gospel" can be taken in two ways. It could refer to the *body* of teaching or tradition of catechetical teaching taught by faithful agents like Epaphras, faithful to Paul's spirit. Toward the end of the first century and into the second this tradition had became standardized or "fixed." This is the meaning of "the Gospel" in the Colossian phrase "truth of the Gospel."

The "truth of the Gospel," with the focus now on "truth," can also refer to the *reception* of this tradition by the audience.[25] The apostolic proclamation is received with comprehension and affirmation by the Colossians. In other words, what is important is not simply understanding the meaning of the apostolic teaching, but its impact on experience in the daily lives of those who "hear" and attend to its meaning. As Eduard Lohse has suggested, "understanding" is intimately linked to "discernment" and "to the probing of things" a Jesus follower "ought to do and leave undone."[26]

Lohse's suggestion, linking understanding to discernment, is supported by the writer's prayer for the Colossians at the beginning of the body of the letter. The author prays that the Colossians "may be filled with the knowledge of God with all spiritual wisdom and discernment" (1:9). If the writer's interest has not become clear, the next verse makes it so. Here the writer prays that the Colossians may "grow in the knowledge of God" (1:10).

Value of Human Experience

The insight from Colossians 1:9-10 concerning the link between experience and truth contrasts with the conventional link between knowledge and truth found in other later New Testament writings, especially the Pastoral Letters (for example, 1 Tim 2:4; 2 Tim 3:7). In the Pastorals the concern is for the preservation of the apostolic teaching. This static formulation is significantly developed in the letter to the Colossians. Noteworthy is the writer's interest in the *experiential reception* of the Gospel's truth in the lives of believers and the impact this has on attitude and conduct.[27] The exemplar of this experiential approach to Gospel teaching is Epaphras. This experiential emphasis noted through "hearing" and "learning" is what the writer means by the knowledge the Colossians "have come to know." Such experiential knowledge has been the writer's principal preoccupation, evident in the early sections of the letter. "Knowledge" concerns the personal and communal appropriation of the truth of salvation, the truth of the Gospel, the life that originates from God, revealed through Christ, into which the Colossians are initiated through baptism. This baptism-triggered life is lived out in their society. Its experiential dimension depends on and links to the Colossians' appropriation of what they understand to be their faith. This is the "wisdom" and "spiritual discernment" the Colossians need, of which the writer speaks in 1:9. Again, the Greek *en* associated with "wisdom" and "spiritual discernment" also affirms their spatial, instrumental, and/or temporal qualities.[28] They are invited to discern "the spirits," the nonpersonal forces that permeate the cosmos.

In 1:9 the adjective "spiritual" modifies "discernment" in the NRSV translation. The adjective could also be associated with "wisdom." "Wisdom" and "discernment" (sometimes translated as "insight") have a rich history in the documents coming from Hellenistic Mediterranean culture. Aristotle regarded them as the most important virtues.[29] They offer ways of comprehending the universe. Colossians links them explicitly to God. They are God's gifts, not the result of human achievement, deriving from God's activity (that is, God's spirit) and related to the human spirit. In this full theological and anthropological sense they are "spiritual."[30] They are also "spiritual" in the sense that they are sensitive to those non-visible entities of the cosmos that are from God. Through the gifts of wisdom and discernment the Colossians come to an intimate, experiential knowledge of God through God's activities (that is, God's spirit, the Holy Spirit). This knowledge is cognitive and deeply relational. It touches the core of the Colossians' humanity and their relationship to God through Christ.

Summary

In summary, the three aspects contained in the two summaries of Epaphras' teaching offered in 1:5b and 1:6b as formulated by the Pauline writer lead to the first explicit mention of Epaphras and his qualities. After this the writer introduces some of the key theological issues the letter will later develop. These concern theological truth and knowledge, humanly experienced and awaiting their completion in the heavenly realm. Noticeable throughout this section are keywords that reveal the writer's interest in the external and internal aspects of the addressees' commitment. As we have already noted, these are concerned with the *content* of what is believed (indicated through the repetition of such nouns as "truth," "knowledge," "wisdom," and "gospel") and the *manner* of believing (suggested by the verbs "hearing," "understanding," "bearing fruit," and "knowing"). This vocabulary expresses Epaphras' educational activity and reflects the primary preoccupation of the writer and the perceived threat to the Colossians' life of faith: an undermining of their appreciation of the central role of Jesus' salvific and cosmic ministry, especially revealed through his death and God's raising him from the dead.

Undergirding this educational activity is Epaphras' agency in strengthening the familial network bonds that characterize the Jesus households of the Colossians. His activity moves them securely into Paul's intimate network zone focused on the Lord Jesus and away from the networks of the letter's opponents. How well Epaphras succeeds in this mission might be conjectured from the writer's flow of ideas in the exposition of Epaphras' teaching centered on the resurrected Jesus (evident in the hymn in Col 1:15-20) and the contrast to what might be considered the letter's polemical core (in Col 2:8, 16-23).[31]

In response to the perceived threat to the Colossians' faith, the Pauline writer develops an educational tactic. We have noted it from the beginning of the letter and in the thanksgiving. It will continue into the body of the letter. This tactic helps to frame the key contribution Epaphras has made in his interpretation of the Pauline tradition on which the writer builds throughout the letter's remaining chapters. In the final greetings of the letter in 4:7-18 the writer returns to mention Epaphras and remind the Colossians of his educational status and authority in the network of other revered Pauline leaders.

CHAPTER 6

Epaphras' Colleagues at Colossae

In the letter's farewell (Col 4:7-18) the writer gathers the names of eight of Paul's network familiar to the Colossians and steeped in Paul's theological vision. These are Tychicus (4:7-9), Onesimus (4:9), Aristarchus (4:10a), Mark (4:10b), Jesus-Justus (4:11), Epaphras (4:12-13), Luke (4:14a), and Demas (4:14b).They confirm their relational ties to the Colossian households by sending their greetings along with Paul's to the Jesus group at Colossae and the other explicitly mentioned Jesus households of the Lycus Valley at Laodicea and Hierapolis. In the final part of the farewell we also learn the names of two Jesus-group leaders in the Lycus Valley: Nympha, a female leader of a Jesus household (4:15), and Archippus (4:17). What emerges in these final verses is the intricacy of the network pattern in which Epaphras is involved. This pattern has personal links to other colleagues in Paul's network, which expands outward to embrace the whole Lycus Valley region represented through the mention of Laodicea and Hierapolis.

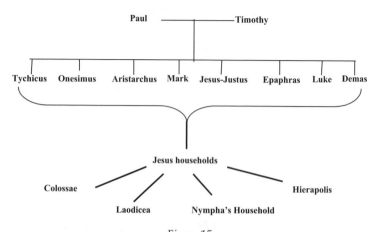

Figure 15
Full Network Pattern as Shown in Colossians 4

Epaphras in Colossians 4:12-13

Among all the descriptions the writer gives of the greeters and the two named recipients, Epaphras receives the most attention. His description repeats and expands on what is said of him in 1:7-8 and confirms his role at Colossae and in the Jesus households in Laodicea and Hierapolis. The writer's emphatic description of Epaphras consolidates his authority among the Jesus groups of the Lycus Valley and his leadership of all those mentioned in the letter's conclusion.

> 12a Epaphras greets you (*aspazomai*),
>   b who is one of you,
>   c a slave of Christ Jesus
>   d always wrestling (*agonizomai*) on your behalf
>   e in prayers
>   f so that you may stand complete
>   g and fulfilled in everything
>   h that is of God's will.

^{13a} For I bear witness to him
  ^b that he has worked hard on your behalf
  ^c and those in Laodicea and Hierapolis. (Col 4:12-13)

As in Philemon, the Pauline writer offers Epaphras' greetings (*aspazomai*) to the Colossians (4:12a). The meaning of such greetings has been noted in Philemon (and discussed in chapter 3 above). The same applies here in the conclusion of the Colossian letter. They communicate the bond of friendship, affection, and solidarity that comes from the shared faith network between Epaphras and the Colossians. The greeting also repeats the conviction of God's attachment to the Colossians celebrated in the letter's opening and thanksgiving. That the greeting comes from Epaphras via Paul underscores the solidarity and fidelity Epaphras has to the Pauline teaching. "Paul" endorses him, ratifies his stance, and can send greetings on his behalf because he knows him so well. More is present, then, in the greeting than simply a warm hello. It reveals the confidence Epaphras has that the Colossians would receive his greetings because of his solidarity with Paul.

Epaphras' Identity with the Colossians (Col 4:12b-c)

The writer also notes that Epaphras is "one of you" (4:12b). He shares the same network complexity as the Colossians. The communion symbolized through the greeting is especially effective because of the explicit, intimate network relationship and identity Epaphras has with the Colossians. He is one of their number, is a Colossian himself, and would be most qualified to represent the concerns and interests of the Colossians before "Paul." Epaphras' Colossian background would also mean that the leadership and theological concerns that have preoccupied "Paul," the Pauline writer, have been authentically engaged through Epaphras' Christ-rooted ideology and educational methodology evident in the letter. Epaphras' standing with the Colossians would mean that his teaching role among them would be well respected. But it also means that the kind of instruction represented in the letter and based on Epaphras' teaching would be most relevant to the addressees. His bond with the Colossians would guarantee that Paul's teaching would have local application. The Colossians can trust Epaphras, learn from his teaching, and live out of it.

The writer also repeats the description of Epaphras as a "slave of Christ Jesus" (4:12c). The difference from 1:7 is that there the writer emphasized Epaphras' slave status, together with Paul's. He is called a "fellow slave." And Epaphras' description *with* Paul (with the use of the *syn-* ["with"] attachment to the Greek word for slave, *doulos*) acted as an authenticating attribute in their union with the resurrected Jesus, on whose behalf they taught and acted. Their bond to Jesus through their obedient commitment to him made them his "slaves." But it also gave Epaphras' proclamation and Pauline interpretation credibility among those in the Colossian Jesus-group households who were slaves. They could identify with those who were slaves like themselves and listen to their proclamation about Christ.

At the end of the letter the writer has no need to emphasize Epaphras' solidarity with Paul as a "fellow slave." This has already been established; Epaphras' authenticity as a Pauline interpreter has been demonstrated throughout the letter. The emphasis now is on Epaphras' solidarity with the letter's addressees. By the Christ-oriented rhetoric of the Pauline writer and the instruction of Epaphras they have moved away from the point of view of the religious opponents with their rituals developed out of a Torah-based perspective and an exaggerated, rigoristic asceticism. The Colossians have been renewed and, like Epaphras, they are now "slaves of Christ." This renewed identity is what cements Epaphras' relationship with them. In the writer's description of Epaphras his identity as "a slave of Christ [Jesus]" follows naturally from his being "one of you." Their identity with each other comes from the union they share with Jesus.

Epaphras' "wrestling" (Col 4:12d)

Epaphras is next noted as "always wrestling on your behalf" (4:12d). This phrase expands further on the solidarity Epaphras shares with the Colossians and his role as one who officially and formerly engages in dialogue with the Pauline tradition on their behalf. This is consistent, too, with the educative role he plays in enabling the Colossians to be "filled with the knowledge of God with all spiritual wisdom and discernment," as noted in 1:9. The Greek word translated as "wrestling" (*agonizomai*) is significant. It suggests that what Epaphras does on behalf of the Colossians before God ("in prayer," as we note next) is not easy, but "agonizing." It reflects the struggle the athlete endures in preparation for the contest. This is the *agonia* of classical Greek, endured by philosophers and athletes in their contest for truth or victory. Significantly, this same idea is employed by Luke in Jesus' "struggle" (agony) in Gethsemane (Luke 22:44). In Luke, as Jesus is about to enter into his passion in which Satan, the tester of loyalty to God, participates, he enters into his *agonia* and seeks to discern God's presence in the midst of the difficulties he is about to endure and the darkness of evil he is about to experience. *Agonia* is the holy one's wrestling with the forces of evil in what appears to be a final conflict of sorts. Something of this same sort of contest is found in the presentation of Epaphras by the writer of the letter to the Colossians. This is especially significant, given the cosmic vista the writer has presented through the letter's theology and its reference to the power the elemental forces seem to have over the Colossians.

Colossians 4:12d is not the only place in this letter, or in the Pauline letters, where *agonizomai* appears. It is also found in 1:29. Here it occurs in the context of a hymn that celebrates the cosmic status of Christ Jesus. The writer affirms that God chose to make Christ known (1:27). The riches of this mystery are expressed in the powerfully deep but simple phrase, "which is Christ in you, the hope of glory." Then the writer continues,

> Him we proclaim, advising every human being and teach-
> ing every human being, in all wisdom, that we might
> present every human being complete in Christ. For this
> also I toil wrestling (*agonizomai*) with all his energy that he
> powerfully inspires in me. For I wish you to know the great
> wrestling (*agōn*) I do for you and all those in Laodicea. (Col
> 1:28–2:1)

The "wrestling" concerns the struggle of "Paul" to allow Christ's
wisdom to guide his activity of bringing all human beings to
their fullness of maturity in Christ. This same "wrestling" shapes
his activity among the Jesus groups in Laodicea. This agenda
affirmed here in "Paul" is echoed in Epaphras' activity affirmed
in Colossians 4:12d, but it is also expanded upon. Epaphras
"wrestles" on behalf of the Colossians in an intercessory ministry
("in prayers," Col 4:12e) that picks up the spirit reflected in
Paul's activity described in Colossians 1:28, namely, bringing
those whom Epaphras serves to a sense of their maturation (Col
4:12f-h). This maturity is what will ultimately enable the Colossians to assess and respond to the seductive aberrations of the
writer's opponents.

"Paul's" Summary of Epaphras' Role (Col 4:13a-c)

The final lines of the Pauline writer's affirmation of Epaphras
(Col 4:13a-c) sum up his role and activity. They draw together
what has emerged in Epaphras' description in the beginning
and end of the letter.

First, the writer reasserts the authority Epaphras holds among
the Colossians and his status as authorized bearer of Paul's
teaching. He is affirmed as the one to whom "Paul" "bears witness." This is a profoundly rich affirmation that can inspire the
letter's audience to trust the kind of education in which Epaphras has been engaged, as noted throughout the letter.

Second, Epaphras is also affirmed as acting among the Colossians with commitment and fidelity (Col 4:13b). They have been

the focus of his activity and their needs have shaped the manner and content of his educational leadership.

Third, the writer affirms the geographical extent of Epaphras' activity. While it has been located in the first instance among the Jesus households of Colossae, it has expanded beyond Colossae to the major centers in which Jesus groups were to be found, namely, Laodicea and Hierapolis (Col 4:13c). The mention of these two other ancient cities is not coincidental and raises in the mind of addressees the implications of what I have identified in chapter 2 as the geographical-spatial network in which Epaphras is involved.

There are several features of the geographical-spatial network of the Lycus Valley that impact upon and shape Epaphras' ministry. Reflection on the three ancient cities of Colossae, Laodicea, and Hierapolis and the Jesus households that existed in them can lead to an appreciation beyond the merely conventional. This

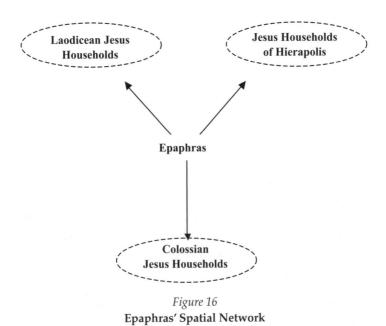

Figure 16
Epaphras' Spatial Network

requires resisting the temptation to retroject our Western experience of religion and Christianity onto Epaphras' world. This
modern approach tends to see religion as a separate part of a
(usually urban) society that takes place in churches or cathedrals
and has little to do with the contemporary marketplace.

As I have already indicated, Epaphras' society was a world
of many deities commanding a range of devotees. Those that
belonged to Jesus groups were part of the complexity that made
up their social networks. Rather than forming a sectarian clique
and simply tolerating "pagan" society, members of these households would represent a wide cross section of Greco-Roman
society, reflecting a mix of social levels.[1] Evidence for this wide
social mix of Jesus-group members is to be found in the list of
names in Colossians 4:7-17: seven are Greek, one is Roman, and
three are Israelite. Only one is female. Their status within the
society of the time would suggest that, of the eleven, four were
or had been slaves. This accords with the suggested ratio of
slaves to free persons during this period.[2]

The interaction of these members with others living in the ancient *polis* would have been more positive than we have hitherto
assumed; they would have actively participated in the economic,
commercial, and political life of their *polis*.[3] They did this while
retaining their fidelity to the Pauline proclamation as explained
to them by Epaphras and possibly while engaging in ongoing
conversation about the fundamental political-religious questions
of their day. It is conceivable that in such conversations some of
the Colossians were lured by the astral, Judeo-folk-mystical, and
ascetic practices of their coreligionists. The classic picture of
"Christian" resistance to a hostile environment through a mono-
lithic form of sectarianism, which has dominated historical analysis until now, needs to be nuanced.[4] In sum, the relational networks
that members of Jesus groups formed with those outside their
in-groups were more positive, open, and relational than has been
previously acknowledged.

Epaphras' activity is clearly located in the Lycus Valley and
within the three explicitly mentioned ancient cities.[5] Their

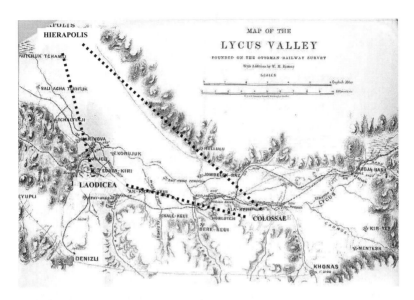

Figure 17
The Lycus Valley

From W. M. Ramsay, *The Church in the Roman Empire before Ad 170 . . . With Maps Etc.* 3d ed. (London: Hodder and Stoughton, 1893). The triangle linking Colossae, Laodicea, and Hierapolis represents the urban-rural connectivity of Jesus groups in the Lycus Valley and part of the spatial network to which Epaphras was connected.

political-religious and political-economic features would have affected Epaphras' instructional style as well as the everyday living of his fellow Jesus followers.

Ancient Colossae

In the ancient world, Colossae was located in the territory of Phrygia, in the Roman province of Asia Minor about two hundred kilometers to the east of Ephesus. Situated on the Lycus River at the foot of Mount Cadmus, Colossae forms one point of a triangle with ancient Laodicea (18 km to the northwest) and Hierapolis (24 km to the north-northeast).[6]

Herodotus called Colossae "a great city in Phrygia."[7] The chronicler Xenophon a century later noted Colossae as a "populous city, both wealthy and large."[8] If Colossae was wealthy, as Xenophon indicates, this might have come from the unique dyed wool of "colossinus" that gave the city its name.[9] Colossae was also strategically located at the junction of the main north-south and east-west trade routes that ran from Pergamum to Attaleia on the Mediterranean coast, and from Apameia to Ephesus on the western coast of Asia Minor. Pliny includes Colossae in a list of famous cities (*oppida celeberrima*).[10] It was therefore geopolitically and economically important during the Persian period and retained its importance in the time of Epaphras, with a symbiotic relationship with Laodicea and Hierapolis. All three were a day's walk from each other, thanks to the Roman road network, and hence were strategically defensible. Current archaeological and inscriptional research on Colossae confirms its importance during the period of Epaphras' activity there.[11]

Ancient Laodicea

The network relationship between the Jesus groups of Colossae and Laodicea was very close. This is indicated by the mention of Laodicea in Colossians 2:1 and the instruction in Colossians 4:16:

> And when this letter has been read among you, have it read also in the church of the Laodiceans; and see that you read also the letter from Laodicea.

The information exchange signified that the subject matter presented through the letter to the Colossians was also relevant to the Laodiceans, for whom Epaphras was also an authority. Laodicea, like Colossae, was involved in the textile and clothing industry through its production of a unique black, soft wool.[12] It was a wealthy urban center that reflected its status through its size, commercial marketplaces, aqueduct, odeon, theaters, temples, basilicas, and one of the most spectacular hippodromes in Asia Minor, second only to that at Aphrodisias.[13] Laodicea's wealth was supplemented by its regional popularity as a commercial, economic, and banking center and its manufacturing of eye medicine.[14]

Ancient Hierapolis

In Epaphras' time Hierapolis was the third mercantile and commercial center in the Lycus Valley geographic network. Its importance lay in purple dyeing, wool washing, and tapestries; it boasted, among many others, a guild of purple dyers.[15] It was a popular destination for those seeking healing at the thermal springs. Hierapolis, like its sibling cities of the Lycus Valley, was polytheistic with a strong cult of the goddess Cybele, Pluto her son, and fertility cults associated with their names. Its famous shrine, known as the "Plutonium," allowed devotees of Pluto to know the alleged route to the underworld.

These all-too-brief summaries of each of these ancient cities seek to offer some feel for the complex social life available to Jesus-group members associated with them. The summaries highlight the various commercial and social associations, their importance and wealth, especially as manufacturing hubs in a textile industry upon which householders of the valley depended—an industry still important today. Some commentators have suggested that the description of Laodicea in Revelation 3:14-22 reflects the geographic and political features unique to the city: water supply, banks, textiles, and medical school. But these features are typical of common realities familiar to the network of Jesus-group households throughout the Lycus Valley.[16] All this suggests something of the complex social network in which Epaphras was involved.

The General Scope of Epaphras' Activity

Though the writer of Colossians reminds the addressees of Epaphras' activity in the *polis*, he has "worked hard" in an area in which these three ancient urban centers existed in symbiosis with the whole region. His service to Jesus-group members was regional rather than urban as we understand it. These cities were not simply network nodal collecting points for transport of the main agricultural and manufacturing products of the valley. They existed in relationship with the rural villages and farming households of the majority who lived outside these cities. This is suggested by Strabo's description of the sheep "around" Laodicea and the quality of wool collected at Colossae. As Strabo describes it, wool production was not limited to one urban center, but was a regional industry:

> The country around Laodicea breeds excellent sheep, re-
> markable not only for the softness of their wool, in which
> they surpass the Milesian flocks, but for their dark or raven
> colour. The Laodiceans derive a large revenue from them,
> as the Colosseni do from their flocks, of a colour of the same
> name.[17]

Plato and Aristotle's understanding of the *polis* as a distinct bounded social entity dominated the way in which the ancient city has been perceived. However, a reconfiguration of this dominant perception occurred in the later Greek period, which expanded this restricted view of the *polis* to embrace the whole "inhabited world" (*oikoumenē*).[18] This expansion, if not hinted at in Strabo's description of the sheep at Laodicea and the wool at Colossae, was obvious in the earlier political conquests of Alexander the Great (356–323 BCE) as he connected cultures and provided a common language, *koinē* Greek, to vanquished tribes. This expanded view of the *polis* was also made explicit in the writings of the historiographer Polybius (ca. 203–120 BCE).

Polybius interpreted cultures, cities, and histories not in separated or dichotomous entities, but as global units composing one great whole network. His interpretation of the history of Rome is typical of this universal outlook: There "can surely be nobody so petty or so apathetic in their outlook," writes Polybius in his reflection on the accomplishments of Rome,

> . . . that they have no desire to discover by what means
> . . . the Romans succeeded in less than fifty-three years
> [from 220 to 167 BCE] in bringing under their rule almost
> the whole of the inhabited world, an achievement which
> is without parallel in human history.[19]

Polybius' conviction that the Romans had united all conquered peoples into one leads him to acknowledge the interrelatedness of the global network in which all peoples, cultural values, and social activities are intertwined. His sense of universal interconnectivity emerges from his conviction about the bond that all history and geography share in an organic whole. This is evident when he writes that

> . . . in earlier times the world's history had consisted, so
> to speak, of a series of unrelated episodes, the origins and
> results of each being as widely separated as their localities,
> but from this point onwards, history becomes an organic
> whole: the affairs of Italy and Africa are interlinked with
> those of Asia and of Greece, and all events bear a relation-
> ship and contribute to a single end.[20]

This leads to a final consideration about Epaphras' authorized instructional role among the Colossians and other Jesus-group households of the Lycus Valley. Polybius' insight into the interconnected and "ecumenical" nature of all temporal and spatial networks was part of Epaphras' philosophical inheritance. It affirmed the broader social nature of his activity in the valley. Certainly this expansive appreciation of Epaphras' instructional activity is reflected in the letter to the Colossians and its presentation of the cosmic and catholic role of Christ, the inspiration for which would have come from Epaphras.

CHAPTER 7

Summarizing Epaphras of Colossae

Epaphras was an agent of the Gospel of God in an area of Asia Minor central to Jesus-movement groups. This was an important place for the growth of Jesus assemblies, even though other places like Rome, Ephesus, Antioch, Jerusalem, Corinth, and Thessalonica have received greater attention.

Despite there being only three New Testament references to him, one from Paul himself in his letter to Philemon and two by a later Pauline writer in the letter to the Colossians, there is a richness to his presentation that allows us to appreciate his authoritative importance to the Jesus households of the Lycus Valley. I have attempted to look closely at the language and expressions used of Epaphras and to unpack their depth within the context of each letter and the writer's intention.

I have also contextualized this more literary and linguistic approach against the backdrop of anthropological and social studies, especially the insights offered by social science concerning social network analysis. We have seen how Epaphras was a member of Paul's network of colleagues and belonged to the intimate zone of relationships, a zone into which Philemon and his household and the Jesus householders of the Lycus Valley were invited. This level of intimacy altered the conventional rules of domestic network engagement and the usual order of the asymmetrical patron-client interchange.

Of further significance in our construction of Epaphras' story were his relational networks. They were complex, broad, and general in scope. They involved people, households, cities, and a multifaceted rural system. This system was affected by several industries and shaped by the power structures of the cities of the Lycus Valley. It mirrored the power dynamics evident in the wider circum-Mediterranean *oikoumenē*. These networks also bridged at least two, possibly three generations of Jesus followers.

As we noticed in Philemon and Colossians, the household pattern of relationships was the template the writers used to affirm the cohesiveness of the members of Jesus groups in the Lycus Valley. Their emphasis on this domestic pattern was obvious from the household language upon which they drew. The authority structures of the household in which they lived were not determined by Greco-Roman convention in which the *paterfamilias*, the male household head, was the authoritative center. Their relationships to each other in Jesus through baptism redefined their kinship relationship in this Jesus household. Even in the household code of Colossians, the traditional code of domestic relationships, we saw how the writer wrestled with the Greco-Roman convention of unilateral power structures in which certain people (husbands, parents, masters) exercised authority over others. This code was reshaped by the premise of God's authority and the role of Jesus in the fictive kinship group. Its teaching about the master-slave relationship was particularly pertinent, given slaves as constitutive members of Jesus households, the "slave" images and metaphors the letter writers employed, and the conjecture of Epaphras' original servile status. His role as instructor among the Colossians might even suggest an earlier role as a *paidagogos*.[1]

By way of conclusion, let me summarize what has emerged from our study of Philemon and Colossians.

Epaphras was a cardinal figure, a symbolic hinge. He ensured the liberating and authentic transition of Paul's Gospel of God from one generation to the next at a time of potential crisis brought on by the death of Paul, and he did this in face of the unsettling teaching of other Jesus followers influenced by astrology, mystical practices, and folk philosophies of Israelite bent. Epaphras lived at a critical moment for the growth in faith of three symbiotic Lycus Valley Jesus groups located at Hierapolis, Laodicea, and Colossae. He became the guarantor of the authenticity of Paul's teaching, the faithful interpreter of this teaching for the next generation of Jesus groups, and the tangible link back to Paul and the apostolic tradition founded on the experience of Jesus Christ. In short, he acted as Paul's interpreter, instructing the Jesus groups of the Lycus Valley. This valley, with its complex commercial, devotional, social, and urban-rural mix, was the geographical heart of Epaphras' network as agent of the Gospel of God. His teaching among the Colossians was particularly crucial, given his authoritative role among them, enhanced by the fact that he was also the founder of their Jesus groups, which he sought to form in the spirit of Paul's teaching relevant for a new moment.

As instructor in the Pauline tradition for the next generation of Jesus followers, Epaphras models an educative practice for subsequent generations, even to our present. This practice emerges from involvement in the lives of people and the complexity of their social reality. It attends to their social issues and seeks to engage these issues in light of a received tradition that has enlivened the faith of previous generations of committed disciples. Epaphras is portrayed as Paul's faithful representative who can authentically engage lifegiving tradition on behalf of the Colossian Jesus groups. This educative dynamic enables those of Epaphras' day to distinguish between what the contemporary theologian Jaroslav Pelikan calls "tradition" and "traditionalism." For Pelikan, "Tradition is the living faith of the dead; traditionalism is the dead faith of the living."[2] Epaphras was committed to stabilizing and supporting the Pauline tradition. It was for this that he was remembered among the Jesus groups at Colossae as their educator.

NOTES

Chapter 1 (pages 1–10)

1. See Bruce J. Malina, *Timothy: Paul's Closest Associate* (Collegeville, MN: Liturgical Press, 2008), "Introduction: Who Is Timothy?"

2. For a summary of the Colossians' Christ-centered variations in the Colossian letter from Paul's genuine letters and a discussion on the language and style of Colossians see Eduard Lohse, *A Commentary on the Epistles to the Colossians and to Philemon* (Philadelphia: Fortress Press, 1971), 84–98, 180–83. On the dating of the letter, its writer and audience, see Margaret Y. MacDonald, *Colossians and Ephesians* (Collegeville: Liturgical Press, 2000), 6–10. A further example of the change in Pauline language seen in Colossians is the shift noted by MacDonald (*Colossians*, p. 41) in Paul's appreciation of "hope" from a temporal-eschatological orientation to a more spatial one.

3. Whether the third or fourth will depend on how one perceives from which generation of Jesus households the letter emerges. Here I draw on Malina, *Timothy*, introduction and chapter 2, where he discusses the four generations of the Jesus group. He locates the writer of Colossians in the fourth generation of Jesus followers. Whether a third- or fourth-generation Jesus follower, the writer acts as Paul's transitional authoritative spokesperson for the next generation of Jesus followers. Epaphras is also the bridge between the second and third generation of Jesus followers at Colossae. As authoritative interpreter of Paul, he presents Paul's teaching to the next (third) generation of believers.

4. The suggestion that Epaphras was responsible for writing Colossians is not new. It first appeared in the nineteenth century with Albert Klöpper,

Der Brief an die Colosser, kritisch untersucht und in seinem Verhältnisse zum paulinischem Lehrbegriff exegetisch und biblisch-theologisch erörtert (Berlin: G. Reimer, 1882). See also Mark Kiley, *Colossians as Pseudepigraphy* (Sheffield: JSOT Press, 1986). The following is a representative sampling of scholars who hold for non-Pauline authorship of Colossians (see Eduard Schweitzer, *Der Brief an die Kolosser,* EKK 12 [Zurich: Benziger; Neukirchen-Vluyn: Neukirchener Verlag, 1976]): Joachim Gnilka, *Der Kolosserbrief* (Freiburg: Herder, 1980); Helmut Merklein, "Paulinische Theologie in der Rezeption des Kolosser- und Epheserbriefes," in *Paulus in den neutestamentlichen Spät-schriften: Zur Paulusrezeption im Neuen Testament,* ed. Karl Kertelge, 25–69 (Freiburg: Herder, 1981); Lohse, *Colossians*; MacDonald, *Colossians*; Raymond F. Collins, *Letters That Paul Did Not Write: The Epistle to the Hebrews and the Pauline Pseudepigrapha* (Collegeville: Liturgical Press, 1994), especially pp. 178–88.

   5. About this leadership crisis, see MacDonald, *Colossians,* 39-41.

   6. See Malina, *Timothy,* "Introduction."

   7. On a social-science view of coworkers as "innovators" and "first adopters" see Bruce J. Malina and John J. Pilch, *Social-Science Commentary on the Letters of Paul* (Minneapolis: Fortress Press, 2006), 348–49.

   8. Kinship transactions and relationships included "genealogy and descent, marriage and divorce, childbearing and rearing, adoption, dowry and inheritance, and social roles." K. C. Hanson and Douglas E. Oakman, *Palestine in the Time of Jesus: Social Structures and Social Conflicts* (Minneapolis: Fortress Press, 1998), 199.

   9. Robert Parker, "Theophoric Names and the History of Greek Religion," in *Greek Personal Names: Their Value as Evidence,* eds. Simon Hornblower and Elaine Matthews, 53–79 (Oxford: Oxford University Press, 2000), at 53.

   10. Joseph A. Fitzmyer, *The Letter to Philemon* (New York: Doubleday, 2000), 123. See Lohse, *Colossians,* 22 n. 80.

   11. While Epaphras' foundational role among the Jesus households of Colossae is well accepted by Pauline scholars, there is some discussion about his role in Laodicea and Hierapolis. See L. Joseph Kreitzer, "Epaphras and Philip: The Undercover Evangelists of Hierapolis," in *"You will be my witnesses": A Festschrift in Honor of the Reverend Dr. Allison A. Trites on the Occasion of His Retirement,* eds. R. Glenn Wooden, Timothy R. Ashley, and Robert S. Wilson, 127–43 (Macon, GA: Mercer University Press, 2003); Alistair Kirkland, "The Beginnings of Christianity in the Lycus Valley. An Exercise in Historical Reconstruction," *Neotestamentica* 29 (1995): 109–24.

   12. For the study of the name of Epaphras I am indebted to the work of Christine Lawrance, *An Investigation of the Names Found in Chapter Four of*

the Letter to the Colossians (unpublished B. Theol [Hon] thesis, Adelaide, South Australia: Flinders University, 2005).

13. Ibid., 106–10.

14. For a helpful cultural summary of slavery in the first century CE see Malina and Pilch, *Social-Science Commentary on the Letters of Paul*, 396–97.

Chapter 2 (pages 11–24)

1. Helpful also are the criteria Bruce Malina offers in employing sociological models to understand biblical texts in "The Social Sciences and Biblical Interpretation," *Interpretation* 37 (1982): 229–42.

2. Moses I. Finley, *Ancient History: Evidence and Models* (London: Chatto & Windus, 1985), 66.

3. For example, evidence of the use of social network analysis is found in the works of Robert A. Atkins, *Egalitarian Community: Ethnography and Exegesis* (Tuscaloosa, AL: University of Alabama Press, 1991); Ronald F. Hock, "'By the gods, it's my one desire to see an actual Stoic': Epictetus' Relations with Students and Visitors in His Personal Network," in *Semeia* 56 (1992): 121–42, as well as the entire issue of L. Michael White, ed., *Social Networks in the Early Christian Environment: Issues and Methods for Social History*, *Semeia* 56 (1991): 1–202; John K. Chow, *Patronage and Power: A Study of Social Networks in Corinth*, JSNT 75 (Sheffield: JSOT Press, 1992); Elizabeth A. Clark, "Elite Networks and Heresy Accusations: Towards a Social Description of the Origenist Controversy," *Semeia* 56 (1992): 79–117; Holland Lee Hendrix, "Benefactor/Patron Networks in the Urban Environment: Evidence from Thessalonica," *Semeia* 56 (1992): 39–58; Rodney Stark, *The Rise of Christianity: A Sociologist Reconsiders History* (Princeton, NJ: Princeton University Press, 1996); Harold Remus, "Voluntary Association and Networks: Aelius Aristides at the Asclepaeion in Pergamum," in *Voluntary Associations in the Graeco-Roman World*, eds. John S. Kloppenborg and Stephen G. Wilson, 146–75 (London and New York: Routledge, 1996); Dennis C. Duling, "The Jesus Movement and Social Network Analysis (Part I: The Spatial Network)," *BTB* 29 (1999): 156–76; idem, "The Jesus Movement and Social Network Analysis (Part II: The Social Network)," *BTB* 30 (2000): 3–15.

4. For a helpful summary of the history of the development of social network analysis see John Scott, *Social Network Analysis: A Handbook* (London: Sage Publications, 2000), 17–37.

5. J. A. Barnes, "Class and Committee in a Norwegian Island Parish," *Human Relations* 7 (1954): 42–43.

6. On the rural application of network analysis theory see Harumi Befu, *Hamlet in a Nation: The Place of Three Japanese Rural Communities in Their Broader Social Context* (Ann Arbor, MI: University Microfilms, 1962); Leopold J. Pospisil, *The Kapauku Papuans of West New Guinea* (New York: Holt, Rinehart and Winston, 1964).

7. The principles enumerated here are adapted from Chow, *Patronage and Power*, 35.

8. Thomas F. Carney, *The Shape of the Past: Models of Antiquity* (Lawrence, KS: Coronado Press, 1975), 171.

9. Adapted from K. C. Hanson and Douglas E. Oakman, *Palestine in the Time of Jesus: Social Structures and Social Conflicts* (Minneapolis: Fortress Press, 1998), 72; Chow, *Patronage and Power*, 33.

10. Material here and following comes from the research on Colossian funerary inscriptions by Alan Cadwallader and available in his *Colossae: The Primary Sources* (forthcoming).

11. William H. Buckler and William M. Calder, eds., *Monumenta Asiae Minoris Antiqua (MAMA)* VI.48 (Manchester: Manchester University Press, 1939), 18. This reading, the one used here, is corrected by Louis Robert and Jeanne Robert, *Bulletin épigraphique* 1979.15 (= *Supplementum Epigraphicum Graecum Volume 29.1391*).

12. *MAMA* VI.47, in Buckler and Calder, *Monumenta*, 17.

13. On the nature of funerary monuments to "impress" see Robert Garland, *The Greek Way of Death* (Ithaca, NY: Cornell University Press, 1985), 109.

14. J. A. Barnes, "Graph theory and social networks: a technical comment on connectedness and connectivity," *Sociology* 3 (1969): 215–32; Jeremy Boissevain, "The Place of Non-Groups in the Social Sciences," *Man* 3 (1968): 542–56; John Scott, "Networks," *The Social Science Encyclopedia*, eds. Adam Kuper and Jessica Kuper, 794–95 (London: Routledge, 1985); J. Clyde Mitchell, "The Concept and Use of Social Networks," in *Social Networks in Urban Situations: Analyses of Personal Relationships in Central African Towns*, ed. idem (Manchester: Manchester University Press, 1969), 1–50.

15. From a contemporary point of view the architectural philosopher Edward Soja emphasizes the importance of "embracing" our spatiality: "Whether we are attempting to deal with the increasing intervention of electronic media in our daily routines; seeking ways to act politically to deal with the growing problems of poverty, racism, sexual discrimination, and environmental degradation; or trying to understand the multiplying geopolitical conflicts around the globe, we are becoming increasingly aware that we are, and always have been, intrinsically spatial beings, active participants in the social construction of our embracing spatialities. Perhaps

more than ever before, a strategic awareness of this collectively created spatiality and its social consequences has become a vital part of making both theoretical and practical sense of our contemporary life-worlds at all scales, from the most intimate to the most global." Edward W. Soja, *Thirdspace: Journeys to Los Angeles and Other Real-and-Imagined Places* (Cambridge, MA: Blackwell, 1996), 1. Also see his *Postmodern Geographies: The Reassertion of Space in Critical Social Theory* (London and New York: Verso, 1989), as quoted in John Inge, *A Christian Theology of Place* (Aldershot, England, and Burlington, VT: Ashgate, 2003), 23.

16. A parallel approach to what I seek to do here in applying the ego-centered network to Philemon and Colossians is the contribution by Duling, ("Jesus Movement, II," 5) to the study of the Jesus movement.

17. Mitchell, "The Concept and Use of Social Networks," 46.

Chapter 3 (pp. 25–39)

1. See, as an example of analysis of the context, situation, and dating of Philemon, Raymond E. Brown, *Introduction to the New Testament* (New York: Doubleday, 1997); Joseph A. Fitzmyer, *The Letter to Philemon* (New York: Doubleday, 2000), 9–11; Joachim Gnilka, *Der Philemonbrief* (Freiburg: Herder, 1982); Eduard Lohse, *A Commentary on the Epistles to the Colossians and to Philemon* (Philadelphia: Fortress Press, 1971). See the work of one scholar on Philemon's location at Colossae in Wilfried Eckey, *Die Briefe des Paulus an die Philipper und an Philemon: Ein Kommentar* (Neukirchen-Vluyn: Neukirchener Verlag, 2006), 153–55.

2. On the variation and spectrum of dependents of an ancient household see Philip A. Harland, *Associations, Synagogues, and Congregations* (Minneapolis: Fortress Press, 2003), 25–53, especially 52.

3. *Gorgias*, 507d.

4. *Gorgias*, 504a.

5. *Politics* I.1.1.

6. For example, Cicero (106–43 BCE) wrote: "Communion is that form of solidarity (*societas*) and partnership of interests (*communicatio*) and the very affection (*caritas*) which exists between human beings. These come into existence as soon as we are born because children are loved by their parents and the whole household is bonded together (*coniungitur*) by the ties of marriage and parenthood" (*De Finibus*, 5. 65).

7. *Politics*, I.2.1-2. It is important to note that Aristotle was not the first to describe household relationships in terms of domination-subordination,

nor did his description define subsequent households. The reality in some cases was quite different. See W. K. Lacey, *The Family in Classical Greece* (London: Thames & Hudson; Ithaca, NY: Cornell University Press, 1968).

8. Bonnie B. Thurston and Judith M. Ryan, *Philippians and Philemon*, SP 10 (Collegeville, MN: Liturgical Press, 2005), 217. "Fictive kinship" expresses the relationships, obligations, and responsibilities between patron and client not based on natural family relationships (K. C. Hanson and Douglas E. Oakman, *Palestine in the Time of Jesus: Social Structures and Social Conflicts* [Minneapolis: Fortress Press, 1998], 80–81). See also Bruce J. Malina and John J. Pilch, *Social-Science Commentary on the Letters of Paul* (Minneapolis: Fortress Press, 2006), 362–63.

9. Thurston and Ryan, *Philippians and Philemon*, 190.

10. Though most commentators consider Onesimus a runaway slave, there are some who hold for the sibling relationship between Onesimus and Philemon. See Allen Dwight Callahan, "Paul's Epistle to Philemon: Toward an Alternative *Argumentum*," *HTR* 86 (1993): 357–76; Margaret M. Mitchell, "John Chrysostom on Philemon: A Second Look," *HTR* 88 (1995): 135–48. For a summary of scholarship on the letter's occasion see Thurston and Ryan, *Philippians and Philemon*, 181–82; Fitzmyer, *Philemon*, 17–19.

11. On this see Fitzmyer, *Philemon*, 124.

12. See Hans Windisch, "ἀσπάζομαι," *TDNT* 1:496–502.

13. Ibid., 499.

14. For this appreciation of the importance of the greetings as a vehicle of the divine presence see, for example, the Lukan perspective evident in Luke 1:29, 40-44; Acts 18:22; 21:7, 19.

15. Sometimes the Greek *chairein* is thought to be the combination of the two Greek words for "grace" (*charis*) and "peace" (*eirenē*).

16. Fitzmyer, *Philemon*, 90–91; idem, *Romans: A New Translation with Introduction and Commentary*, AB 33 (New York: Doubleday, 1993), 228, 239.

17. Fitzmyer, *Romans*, 228.

18. Malina and Pilch, *Social-Science Commentary*, 356–57.

19. M. Luther Stirewalt, *Paul, the Letter Writer* (Grand Rapids, MI: Eerdmans, 2003), 92–95.

20. Abraham J. Malherbe, *Ancient Epistolary Theorists* (Atlanta, GA: Scholars Press, 1988), 12.

21. For more on the "friendly letter" see Stanley K. Stowers, *Letter Writing in Greco-Roman Antiquity* (Philadelphia: Westminster, 1986), 43–44, 71–76.

22. Demetrius, *On Style* 225f., as quoted by Malherbe, *Ancient Epistolary Theoriests*, 58.

23. Helpful for a cultural appreciation of the relationship between *koinōnia* and *societas* is Bruce J. Malina, "The Social World Implied in the Letters of the Christian Bishop-Martyr (Named Ignatius of Antioch)," in *Society of Biblical Literature Seminar Papers, Vol II*, ed. Paul J. Achtemeier (Missoula, MT: Scholars Press, 1978), 71–119.

Chapter 4 (pages 41–54)

1. The association of the work of the *synergos* with the explicit proclamation of the Gospel is certainly the emphasis found in 2 Corinthians 8:23. See BDAG, 969; Wolf-Henning Ollrog, *Paulus und seine Mitarbeiter: Untersuchungen zu Theorie und Praxis der paulinischen Mission* (Neukirchen-Vluyn: Neukirchener Verlag, 1979), 67.

2. Frederick W. Danker, *A Greek-English Lexicon of the New Testament and Other Early Christian Literature*, 3rd ed. (Chicago: University of Chicago Press, 2000), 969.

3. Helpful overviews of slavery in the ancient world and the early Jesus movement include Keith R. Bradley, *Slavery and Society at Rome* (Cambridge: Cambridge University Press, 1994); Jennifer A. Glancy, *Slavery in Early Christianity* (New York: Oxford University Press, 2002); J. Albert Harrill, *Slaves in the New Testament: Literary, Social and Moral Dimensions* (Minneapolis: Fortress Press, 2005); W. S. Johnson, "Empire and Order: The Gospel and Same-Gender Relationships," *BTB* 37, no. 4 (2007): 161–73: Bruce J. Malina and John J. Pilch, *Social-Science Commentary on the Letters of Paul* (Minneapolis: Fortress Press, 2006).

4. Malina and Pilch, *Social-Science Commentary*, 396.

5. Dale B. Martin, *Slavery as Salvation: The Metaphor of Slavery in Pauline Christianity* (New Haven and London: Yale University Press, 1990).

6. Malina and Pilch, *Social-Science Commentary*, 396.

7. Margaret Y. MacDonald, *Colossians and Ephesians*, SP 17 (Collegeville, MN: Liturgical Press, 2000), 39.

8. Joseph A. Fitzmyer, *The Letter to Philemon*, AB 34C (New York: Doubleday, 2000), 31.

9. In Exodus 14:31; 1 Samuel 3:10; 1 Kings 8:66; Job 1:8; Psalm 31:16; Isaiah 43:10; 53:11; Jeremiah 33:21; Ezekiel 34:24; Zechariah 3:8.

10. On the senses of Paul's description of Epaphras as "my fellow prisoner" see Marcus Barth and Helmut Blanke, *The Letter to Philemon. A New Translation and Commentary* (Grand Rapids, MI: Eerdmans, 2000), 496. I consider that the "imprisonment" of Paul and Epaphras is not just a literary

or rhetorical device, and, contra Fitzmyer, "the mention of [Paul's] status [as imprisoned] has to be taken at face value" (Fitzmyer, *Philemon*, 84).

11. On Paul's use of "being chained" see Gerhard Kittel, "αἰχμάλωτος, κτλ.," *TDNT* 1:195–97, especially 197.

12. Bonnie B. Thurston and Judith M. Ryan, *Philippans and Philemon,* SP 10 (Collegeville, MN: Liturgical Press, 2005), 256; see also Hebrews 13:13; *TDNT* 1:196–97.

13. Thurston and Ryan, *Philippians and Philemon,* 218.

14. For a popular summary of the dating of the genuine letters of Paul see Raymond E. Brown, *Introduction to the New Testament,* ABRL (New York: Doubleday, 1997), 428–29, 432–35, who suggests that Philemon was written about 55 CE and Romans about 57/58 CE. This is the dating from which I shall work.

15. Brendan Byrne, *Romans,* SP 6 (Collegeville, MN: Liturgical Press, 1996), 453, considers Paul's relatives as members of his fictive kinship group.

16. Malina and Pilch, *Social-Science Commentary,* 222.

17. On the definition of "apostle" see Byrne, *Romans,* 38–41.

18. Ibid. (following Dunn), 453.

Chapter 5 (pages 55–78)

1. On the crisis in leadership that resulted from Paul's death see Margaret Y. MacDonald, *Colossians and Ephesians,* SP 17 (Collegeville, MN: Liturgical Press, 2000), 7–8, and her earlier work, *The Pauline Churches: A Socio-Historical Study of Institutionalization in the Pauline and Deutero-Pauline Writings* (Cambridge: Cambridge University Press, 1988). More will be said of this crisis and Epaphras' role below.

2. See the discussion of this thesis by Martin Troy, "'But Let Everyone Discern the Body of Christ' (Colossians 2:17)," *JBL* 114 (1995): 249–55, who argues that the writer is building up a positive argument rather than drawing a contrast between what the opponents teach (which is a "shadow") and what the Colossians are expected to do (in preparing for what is to come in Christ). In an unpublished paper, Elizabeth Prior, "Colossians 2:16-19," proposes that the phrase translated above as "but the body is of Christ" can arguably also be the subject governing the verb of judgment. In other words, the body of Christ also becomes the judging agent of what is acceptable in the cultic practice of the Jesus followers. The body of Christ can judge, in contrast to those others who cast judgment on the Colossians. Herman N. Ridderbos, *Paul: An Outline of His Theology* (Grand Rapids, MI:

Eerdmans, 1975), 377, hints at the link between "body" and the "Body of Christ" throughout Colossians and Ephesians. This link could arguably be sustained in 2:17.

3. MacDonald, *Colossians and Ephesians,* 105. Taking a different tack, Robert M. Royalty, "Dwelling on Visions: On the Nature of the So-called 'Colossians Heresy,'" *Bib* 83 (2002): 329–57, argues that, besides being dated post-70 CE, Colossians was composed in response to an emphasis on apocalyptic prophetic activity and the visions of heavenly worship encouraged by John, writer of the book of Revelation.

4. Victor P. Furnish, "Colossians, Epistle to the," *Anchor Bible Dictionary* (New York: Doubleday, 1992) 1:1090–96, at 1092, and MacDonald, *Colossians and Ephesians*, 112–13, offer helpful summaries of the scholarly discussion. Clinton E. Arnold prefers to interpret the expression "worship of angels" as part of the writer's condemnation of magical practice in which angels were invoked as protection from evil; see his *The Colossian Syncretism: The Interface between Christianity and Folk Belief at Colossae* (Tübingen: J. C. B. Mohr, 1995).

5. For the recognition of asceticism's multifaceted nature in the Greco-Roman world see Vincent L. Wimbush, ed., *Ascetic Behavior in Greco-Roman Antiquity: A Sourcebook* (Minneapolis: Fortress Press, 1990), especially 20–21; and Richard Valantasis and Vincent L. Wimbush, eds., *Asceticism* (New York: Oxford University Press, 1995).

6. See Eduard Lohse's interpretation of the syncretistic position of the writer's opponents as he gleans the main points of their philosophy from quotations and catchwords in the letter: *Colossians and Philemon: A Commentary on the Epistles to the Colossians and to Philemon*, trans. William R. Poehlmann and Robert J. Karris, ed. Helmut Koester, Hermeneia (Philadelphia: Fortress Press, 1971), 127–31.

7. Mary Rose D'Angelo, "Colossians," in Elisabeth Schüssler Fiorenza, ed., *Searching the Scriptures 2: A Feminist Commentary* (New York: Crossroad, 1994), 319–20, presumes that the stance of the writer's opponents was not less Christocentric. Their emphasis lay rather on ascetic practice and visions. See also MacDonald, *Colossians and Ephesians*, 116.

8. Arnold, *Colossian Syncretism*, 60.

9. Several suggestions have been offered as to the exact nature of the "worship of angels" the letter opposes and the identity of the Colossian opponents, with proposals ranging from Gnostics to Anatolian syncretists. For a summary see Arnold, *Colossian Syncretism*, 1–3.

10. MacDonald, *Colossians and Ephesians*, 11–12.

11. I recognize that the use of the contemporary term "education" as a description for what the Colossian writer is alluding to is, of course,

anachronistic. Still, given the cultural and chronological gap between the Colossians' world and our own, the aims of the letter's writer and those of religious educators today seem parallel: to make sense of the present in light of the inherited faith wisdom of the past. The word "education" is contemporary; a community's desire to instruct and nurture people in the core sustaining beliefs and practices of its religious tradition is ancient. For a summary of educational tradition and history in the Mediterranean world before Jesus see James L. Crenshaw, *Education in Ancient Israel: Across the Deadening Silence* (New York, London, Toronto, Sydney, Auckland: Doubleday, 1998).

12. For a study of the cosmic Christology of Colossians and its implications for contemporary ecological issues see Michael Trainor, "The Cosmic Christology of Colossians 1:15-20 in the Light of Contemporary Ecological Issues," *ABR* 53 (2005): 54–69.

13. On the variation of slave status in the Greco-Roman world see Dale B. Martin, *Slavery as Salvation: The Metaphor of Slavery in Pauline Christianity* (New Haven and London: Yale University Press, 1990), 1–49.

14. For a summary of the slave issue at Colossae and scholarship on it see MacDonald, *Colossians and Ephesians*, 161–69. On Paul's rhetoric in 1 Corinthians 7:22-23 see Martin, *Slavery as Salvation*, 60–68.

15. MacDonald, *Colossians and Ephesians*, 164.

16. Ibid.

17. Ibid., 107, drawing on the work of Victor Turner and his concept of *communitas*.

18. On the conduct of masters toward their slaves in the Colossian Jesus households see Margaret Y. MacDonald, "Slavery, Sexuality and House Churches: A Reassessment of Colossians 3.18–4.1 in Light of New Research on the Roman Family," *NTS* 53 (2007): 94–113.

19. Bruce J. Malina and John J. Pilch, *Social-Science Commentary on the Letters of Paul* (Minneapolis: Fortress Press, 2006), 292.

20. On the meaning of *diakonos* and its cognates see John N. Collins, *Diakonia: Reinterpreting the Ancient Sources* (New York: Oxford University Press, 1990).

21. On this textual variation see Lohse, *Colossians and Philemon*, 23, n. 90. Lohse, like many contemporary commentators, favors "on behalf of us" and suggests that the change to "on behalf of you" was due to the influence of Colossians 4:12.

22. MacDonald, *Colossians and Ephesians*, 38.

23. Jerome Murphy-O'Connor explores Epaphras' influence on the Colossian hymn in "Tradition and Redaction in Col 1:15-20," *RB* 102 (1995): 231–41.

24. Lohse, *Colossians and Philemon*, 18–21.

25. MacDonald, *Colossians and Ephesians*, 38; Lohse, *Colossians and Philemon*, 18–19.

26. Lohse, *Colossians and Philemon*, 20.

27. For more on the link between "knowledge" and "experience" see *TDNT* 1:706–07; Lohse, *Colossians and Philemon*, nn. 71-75: as connected to correct teaching that affects life.

28. For a discussion of Epaphras' educational ministry in bringing the Gospel into positive dialogue with the Colossian culture, especially as represented by the Pythagoreans and Platonists, see Helmut Renard and Christian Tauchner, "Something in the Air," *International Review of Mission* 91 (2002): 52–61.

29. Aristotle, *Nicomachean Ethics* 1, 13, 1103a; Lohse, *Colossians and Philemon*, 26.

30. The link between being "spiritual" and the ability to discern is supported by MacDonald, *Colossians and Ephesians*, 48; Lohse, *Colossians and Philemon*, 27. This is a positive human capacity, originating from God, that enables the Colossians to interpret their world with an awareness of the "spirit" realities that permeate the cosmos.

31. Richard E. DeMaris, *The Colossian Controversy: Wisdom in Dispute at Colossae* (Sheffield: JSOT Press, 1994), 41–97.

Chapter 6 (pages 79–91)

1. Philip A. Harland, *Associations, Synagogues, and Congregations* (Minneapolis: Fortress Press, 2003), 51.

2. Christine Lawrance, *An Investigation of the Names Found in Chapter Four of the Letter to the Colossians*, (unpublished B. Theol [Hon] thesis, Adelaide, South Australia: Flinders University, 2005), 137.

3. This is the main thesis of Harland, *Associations*, especially 213–37.

4. Ibid., 8–20.

5. For a discussion of the key leaders responsible for the foundation of the Jesus households in Colossae, Laodicea, and Hierapolis, see Alistair Kirkland, "The Beginnings of Christianity in the Lycus Valley. An Exercise in Historical Reconstruction," *Neotestamentica* 29 (1995): 109–24.

6. Mount Cadmus, known today by its Turkish name, Honaz Dagi, has an elevation of 2,528 meters.

7. Herodotus, *Histories* 7.30.1.

8. Xenophon, *Anabasis* 1.2.6.

9. According to Strabo, *Geography* 12.8.16; Pliny, *Hist. Nat.* 11.51.

10. Pliny, *Hist. Nat.* 5.145.

11. This work is being undertaken by Pamukkale University archaeologists from Turkey and researchers from Flinders University School of Theology, South Australia. The present state of research on Colossae is well summed up in the comprehensive CD-ROM by Alan H. Cadwallader et al., *Colossae in Time and Space: Linking to an Ancient City* (Adelaide: Adelaide College of Divinity, 2007). For a summary of the history of archaeological research on Colossae see Alan H. Cadwallader and Michael Trainor, "The rise and fall of the European recovery of the Ancient site of Colossae," in *Uluslararasi Denizli ve Çevresi Tarih ve Kültür Sempozyrumu [International Symposium on the History and Culture of Denizli and Its Surroundings 2]* (Denizli: Pamukkale University, 2007), 73–79.

12. Strabo, *Geography,* 12.8.16

13. On the most recent archaeological work on Laodicea consult Celal Şimşek, *Laodikeia (Laodikeia ad Lycum)* (Istanbul: Ege yayınları, 2007).

14. See Tenney Frank, ed., *An Economic Survey of Ancient Rome,* 5 vols. (Baltimore: Johns Hopkins University Press, 1931–40), 4:821; Colin J. Hemer, *The Letters to the Seven Churches of Asia in Their Local Setting* (London: JSOT Press, 1986), 182.

15. Frank, ed., *Economic Survey,* 4:820.

16. This wider valley application of the references to Laodicea is argued by Craig Koester, "The Message to Laodicea and the Problem of Its Local Context: A Study of the Imagery in Rev 3.14–22," *New Testament Studies* 49 (2003): 407–24.

17. *Geography,* 12.8.16.

18. David Inglis and Roland Robertson, "Beyond the Gates of the *Polis*: Reconfiguring Sociology's Ancient Inheritance," *Journal of Classical Sociology* 4 (2004): 165–89.

19. Translation adapted from Polybius, *The Rise of the Roman Empire,* trans. Ian Scott-Kilvert; selected with an introduction by Frank W. Walbank (Harmondsworth and New York: Penguin, 1979), 41.

20. Adapted from ibid., 43.

Chapter 7 (pages 93–95)

1. Christine Lawrance, *An Investigation of the Names Found in Chapter Four of the Letter to the Colossians,* (unpublished B. Theol [Hon] thesis, Adelaide, South Australia: Flinders University, 2005), 114.

2. Jaroslav Pelikan, *The Vindication of Tradition* (New Haven: Yale University Press, 1986), 65.

BIBLIOGRAPHY

Arnold, Clinton E. *The Colossian Syncretism: The Interface between Christianity and Folk Belief at Colossae.* Tübingen: J. C. B. Mohr, 1995.

Atkins, Robert A. *Egalitarian Community: Ethnography and Exegesis.* Tuscaloosa, AL: University of Alabama Press, 1991.

Barnes, J. A. "Class and Committee in a Norwegian Island Parish." *Human Relations* 7 (1954): 42–43.

———. "Graph Theory and Social Networks: A Technical Comment on Connectedness and Connectivity." *Sociology* 3 (1969): 215–32

Barth, Marcus, and Helmut Blanke. *The Letter to Philemon. A New Translation and Commentary.* Eerdmans Critical Commentary. Grand Rapids, MI: Eerdmans, 2000.

Befu, Harumi. *Hamlet in a Nation: The Place of Three Japanese Rural Communities in Their Broader Social Context.* Ann Arbor, MI: University Microfilms, 1962.

Boissevain, Jeremy. "Networks." *The Social Science Encyclopedia.* Edited by Adam Kuper and Jessica Kuper. London: Routledge, 1985.

———. "The Place of Non-Groups in the Social Sciences." *Man* 3 (1968): 542–56.

Bradley, Keith R. *Slavery and Society at Rome.* Cambridge: Cambridge University Press, 1994.

Brown. Raymond E. *Introduction to the New Testament.* Anchor Bible Reference Library. New York: Doubleday, 1997.

Buckler, William H., and William M. Calder, eds. *Monumenta Asiae Minoris Antiqua.* Volume 6. Manchester: Manchester University Press, 1939.

Byrne, Brendan. *Romans.* Sacra Pagina 6. Collegeville, MN: Liturgical Press, 1996.

Cadwallader, Alan H., et al. *Colossae in Time and Space: Linking to an Ancient City*. CD-ROM. Adelaide: Adelaide College of Divinity, 2007.

———, and Michael Trainor. "The Rise and Fall of the European Recovery of the Ancient Site of Colossae." In *Uluslararasi Denizli ve Çevresi Tarih ve Kültür Sempozyrumu [International Symposium on the History and Culture of Denizli and Its Surroundings 2]*, 73–79. Denizli: Pamukkale University, 2007.

Callahan, Allen Dwight. "Paul's Epistle to Philemon: Toward an Alternative *Argumentum*." *Harvard Theological Review* 86 (1993): 357–76.

Carney, Thomas F. *The Shape of the Past: Models of Antiquity*. Lawrence, KS: Coronado Press, 1975.

Chow, John K. *Patronage and Power: A Study of Social Networks in Corinth*. JSNT 75. Sheffield: JSOT Press, 1992.

Clark, Elizabeth A. "Elite Networks and Heresy Accusations: Towards a Social Description of the Origenist Controversy." *Semeia* 56 (1992): 79–117.

Collins, John N. *Diakonia: Reinterpreting the Ancient Sources*. New York: Oxford University Press, 1990.

Collins, Raymond F. *Letters That Paul Did Not Write: The Epistle to the Hebrews and the Pauline Pseudepigrapha*. Collegeville, MN: Liturgical Press, 1994.

Crenshaw, James L. *Education in Ancient Israel: Across the Deadening Silence*. New York, London, Toronto, Sydney, Auckland: Doubleday, 1998.

Danker, Frederick W. *A Greek-English Lexicon of the New Testament and Other Early Christian Literature*. 3rd ed. Chicago: University of Chicago Press, 2000.

D'Angelo, Mary Rose. "Colossians." In *Searching the Scriptures 2: A Feminist Commentary*. Edited by Elisabeth Schüssler Fiorenza, 319–20. New York: Crossroad, 1994.

DeMaris, Richard E. *The Colossian Controversy: Wisdom in Dispute at Colossae*. JSNTSup 96. Sheffield: JSOT Press, 1994.

Duling, Dennis C. "The Jesus Movement and Social Network Analysis (Part I: The Spatial Network)." *Biblical Theology Bulletin* 29 (1999): 156–76.

———. "The Jesus Movement and Social Network Analysis (Part II: The Social Network)." *Biblical Theology Bulletin* 30 (2000): 3–15.

Eckey, Wilfried. *Die Briefe des Paulus an die Philipper und an Philemon: Ein Kommentar.* Neukirchen-Vluyn: Neukirchener Verlag, 2006.

Finley, Moses I. *Ancient History: Evidence and Models.* London: Chatto & Windus, 1985.

Fitzmyer, Joseph A. *The Letter to Philemon.* AB 34C. New York: Doubleday, 2000.

Frank, Tenney, ed. *An Economic Survey of Ancient Rome.* Baltimore: Johns Hopkins University Press, 1938.

Furnish, Victor P. "Colossians, Epistle to the." *The Anchor Bible Dictionary.* New York: Doubleday, 1992, 1:1092.

Garland, Robert. *The Greek Way of Death.* Ithaca, NY: Cornell University Press, 1985.

Glancy, Jennifer A. *Slavery in Early Christianity.* New York: Oxford University Press, 2002.

Gnilka, Joachim. *Der Kolosserbrief.* HTKNT 10/1. Freiburg: Herder, 1980.

———. *Der Philemonbrief.* HTKNT 10/4. Freiburg: Herder, 1982.

Hanson, K. C., and Douglas E. Oakman. *Palestine in the Time of Jesus: Social Structures and Social Conflicts.* Minneapolis: Fortress Press, 1998.

Harland, Philip A. *Associations, Synagogues, and Congregations.* Minneapolis: Fortress Press, 2003.

Harrill, J. Albert. *Slaves in the New Testament: Literary, Social and Moral Dimensions.* Minneapolis: Fortress Press, 2006.

Hemer, Colin J. *The Letters to the Seven Churches of Asia in Their Local Setting.* JSOTSup 11. Sheffield: JSOT Press, 1986.

Hendrix, Holland Lee. "Benefactor/Patron Networks in the Urban Environment: Evidence from Thessalonica." *Semeia* 56 (1992): 39–58.

Hock, Ronald F. "'By the gods, it's my one desire to see an actual Stoic': Epictetus' Relations with Students and Visitors in His Personal Network." *Semeia* 56 (1991): 121–42.

Hornblower, Simon, and Elaine Mathews, eds. *Greek Personal Names: Their Value and Existence.* Oxford and New York: Published for the British Academy by Oxford University Press, 2000.

Inge, John. *A Christian Theology of Place.* Aldershot, Hampshire, and Burlington, VT: Ashgate, 2003.

Inglis, David, and Roland Robertson. "Beyond the Gates of *Polis*: Reconfiguring Sociology's Ancient Inheritance." *Journal of Classical Sociology* 4 (2004): 165–89.

Johnson, W. S. "Empire and Order: The Gospel and Same-Gender Relationships." *Biblical Theology Bulletin* 37 no. 4 (2007): 161–73.

Kittel, Gerhard. "αἰχμάλωτος, κτλ." *Theological Dictionary of the New Testament.* Grand Rapids, MI: Eerdmans, 1965, 1:195–97.

Kiley, Mark. *Colossians as Pseudepigraphy.* Sheffield: JSOT Press, 1986.

Kirkland, Alistair. "The Beginnings of Christianity in the Lycus Valley. An Exercise in Historical Reconstruction." *Neotestamentica* 29 (1995): 109–24.

Kloppenborg, John S., and Stephen G. Wilson, eds. *Voluntary Associations in the Graeco-Roman World.* London and New York: Routledge, 1996.

Koester, Craig. "The Message to Laodicea and the Problem of Its Local Context: A Study of the Imagery in Rev 3.14–22." *New Testament Studies* 49 (2003): 407–24.

Kreitzer, L. Joseph. "Epaphras and Philip: The Undercover Evange-lists of Hierapolis." In *"You will be my witnesses": A Festschrift in Honor of the Reverend Dr. Allison A. Trites on the Occasion of His Retirement.* Edited by R. Glenn Wooden, Timothy R. Ashley, and Robert S Wilson, 127–43. Macon, GA: Mercer University Press, 2003.

Kuper, Adam, and Jessica Kuper, eds. *The Social Science Encyclopedia.* London: Routledge, 1985.

Lawrance, Christine. *An Investigation of the Names Found in Chapter Four of the Letter to the Colossians.* Unpublished B. Theol (Hon) thesis. Adelaide, South Australia: Flinders University, 2005.

Lohse, Eduard. *Colossians and Philemon: A Commentary on the Epistles to the Colossians and to Philemon.* Translated by William R. Poehlmann and Robert J. Karris. Edited by Helmut Koester. Hermeneia. Philadelphia: Fortress Press, 1971.

MacDonald, Margaret Y. *Colossians and Ephesians.* Sacra Pagina 17. Collegeville, MN: Liturgical Press, 2000.

———. *The Pauline Churches: A Socio-Historical Study of Institutionalization in the Pauline and Deutero-Pauline Writings.* Cambridge: Cambridge University Press, 1988.

———. "Slavery, Sexuality and House Churches: A Reassessment of Colossians 3.18–4.1 in Light of New Research on the Roman Family." *New Testament Studies* 53 (2007): 94–113.

Malherbe, Abraham J. *Ancient Epistolary Theorists.* Atlanta: Scholars Press, 1988.

Malina, Bruce J. "The Social World Implied in the Letters of the Christian Bishop-Martyr (Named Ignatius of Antioch)." In *Society of Biblical Literature Seminar Papers. Vol II.* Edited by Paul J. Achtemeier, 71–119. Missoula, MT: Scholars Press, 1978.

———. *Timothy: Paul's Chief Coworker.* Collegeville, MN: Liturgical Press, 2008.

———, and John J. Pilch. *Social-Science Commentary on the Letters of Paul.* Minneapolis: Fortress Press, 2006.

Martin, Dale B. *Slavery as Salvation: The Metaphor of Slavery in Pauline Christianity.* New Haven and London: Yale University Press, 1990.

Martin, Troy. "'But Let Everyone Discern the Body of Christ' (Colossians 2:17)." *Journal of Biblical Literature* 114 (1995): 249–55.

Merklein, Helmut. "Paulinische Theologie in der Rezeption des Kolosser- und Epheserbriefes." In *Paulus in den neutestamentlichen Spätschriften: Zur Paulusrezeption im Neuen Testament.* QD 89. Edited by Karl Kertelege, 25–69. Freiburg: Herder, 1981.

Mitchell, J. Clyde. "The Concept and Use of Social Networks." In *Social Networks in Urban Situations: Analyses of Personal Relationships in Central African Towns.* Edited by J. Clyde Mitchell, 1–50. Manchester: Manchester University Press, 1969.

Mitchell, Margaret M. "John Chrysostom on Philemon: A Second Look." *Harvard Theological Review* 88 (1995): 135–48.

Murphy-O'Connor, Jerome. "Tradition and Redaction in Col 1:15-20." *Revue Biblique* 102 (1995): 231–41.

Ollrog, Wolf-Henning. *Paulus und seine Mitarbeiter: Untersuchungen zu Theorie und Praxis der paulinischen Mission.* Neukirchen-Vluyn: Neukirchener Verlag, 1979.

Parker, Robert. "Theophoric Names and the History of Greek Religion." In *Greek Personal Names: Their Value as Evidence.* Edited by Simon Hornblower and Elaine Matthews, 53–80. Oxford and New York: Published for the British Academy by Oxford University Press, 2000.

Pelikan, Jaroslav. *The Vindication of Tradition.* New Haven: Yale University Press, 1986.

Polybius. *The Rise of the Roman Empire.* Translated by Ian Scott-Kilvert. Selected with an introduction by Frank W. Walbank. Harmondsworth and New York: Penguin, 1979.

Pospisil, Leopold J. *The Kapauku Papuans of West New Guinea*. Case Studies in Cultural Anthropology. New York: Holt, Rinehart and Winston, 1964.

Remus, Harold. "Voluntary Association and Networks: Aelius Aristides at the Asclepaeion in Pergamum." In *Voluntary Associations in the Graeco-Roman World*. Edited by John S. Kloppenborg and Stephen G. Wilson, 146–75. London and New York: Routledge, 1996.

Renard, Helmut, and Christian Tauchner. "Something in the Air." *International Review of Mission* 91 (2002): 52–61.

Ridderbos, Herman N. *Paul: An Outline of His Theology*. Translated by John Richard DeWitt. Grand Rapids, MI: Eerdmans, 1975.

Royalty, Robert M. "Dwelling on Visions: On the Nature of the So-called 'Colossians Heresy.'" *Biblica* 83 (2002): 329–57.

Schüssler Fiorenza, Elisabeth, ed. *Searching the Scriptures 2: A Feminist Commentary*. New York: Crossroad, 1994.

Scott, John. *Social Network Analysis: A Handbook*. London and Newbury Park, CA: SAGE Publications, 2000.

Şimşek, Celal. *Laodikeia (Laodikeia ad Lycum)*. Istanbul: Ege yayınları, 2007.

Soja, Edward W. *Postmodern Geographies: The Reassertion of Space in Critical Social Theory*. London and New York: Verso, 1989.

———. *Thirdspace: Journeys to Los Angeles and Other Real-and-Imagined Places*. Malden, MA: Blackwell, 1996.

Stark, Rodney. *The Rise of Christianity: A Sociologist Reconsiders History*. Princeton, NJ: Princeton University Press, 1996.

Stirewalt, M. Luther. *Paul, the Letter Writer*. Grand Rapids, MI: Eerdmans, 2003.

Stowers, Stanley K. *Letter Writing in Greco-Roman Antiquity*. Philadelphia: Westminster, 1986.

Swete, Henry Barclay. *The Apocalypse of St John*. London: MacMillan and Co., 1906.

Thurston, Bonnie B., and Judith M. Ryan. *Philippans and Philemon*. Sacra Pagina 10. Collegeville, MN: Liturgical Press, 2005.

Trainor, Michael. "The Cosmic Christology of Colossians 1:15-20 in the Light of Contemporary Ecological Issues." *Australian Biblical Review* 53 (2005): 54–69.

Valantasis, Richard, and Vincent L. Wimbush, eds. *Asceticism*. New York: Oxford University Press, 1995.

White, L. Michael, ed. *Social Networks in the Early Christian Environment: Issues and Methods for Social History*. *Semeia* 56 (1991): 1–202.

Windisch, Hans. "ἀσπάζομαι." *Theological Dictionary of the New Testament*. Grand Rapids, MI: Eerdmans, 1965, 1:496–502.

Wimbush, Vincent L., ed. *Ascetic Behavior in Greco-Roman Antiquity: A Sourcebook*. Minneapolis: Fortress Press, 1990.

INDEX OF PERSONS AND SUBJECTS

INDEX OF BIBLICAL SOURCES